SCARCITY AND MODERNITY

SCARCITY AND MODERNITY

NICHOLAS XENOS

Routledge
London and New York

First published 1989
by Routledge
11 New Fetter Lane, London EC4P 4EE
29 West 35th Street, New York, NY 10001

In Trump Mediaeval 10/13pt.
Disc conversion by Columns of Reading.
Printed in Great Britain by TJ Press (Padstow) Ltd, Padstow, Cornwall

British Library Cataloguing in Publication Data
Xenos, Nicholas
    Scarcity and modernity.
    1. Culture. Modernism
    I. Title
    306
    ISBN 0 415 01516 2
    0415 04376 X (pbk)

Library of Congress Cataloging in Publication Data
Xenos, Nicholas
    Scarcity and modernity/Nicholas Xenos.
        p. cm.
    Includes index.
    ISBN 0 415 01516 2
    0 415 04376 X (pbk)
    1. Scarcity. 2. Natural resources. 3. Supply and demand.
    HB199.X46   1989
    333.7 — dc19

To my parents,
to Becca,
and
to George

At the end of three days, moving southward, you come upon Anastasia, a city with concentric canals watering it and kites flying over it. I should now list the wares that can profitably be bought here: agate, onyx, chrysoprase, and other varieties of chalcedony; I should praise the flesh of the golden pheasant cooked here over fires of seasoned cherry wood and sprinkled with much sweet marjoram; and tell of the women I have seen bathing in the pool of a garden and who sometimes – it is said – invite the stranger to disrobe with them and chase them in the water. But with all this, I would not be telling you the city's true essence; for while the description of Anastasia awakens desires one at a time only to force you to stifle them, when you are in the heart of Anastasia one morning your desires waken all at once and surround you. The city appears to you as a whole where no desire is lost and of which you are a part, and since it enjoys everything you do not enjoy, you can do nothing but inhabit this desire and be content. Such is the power, sometimes called malignant, sometimes benign, that Anastasia, the treacherous city, possesses; if for eight hours a day you work as a cutter of agate, onyx, chrysoprase, your labor which gives form to desire takes from desire its form, and you believe you are enjoying Anastasia wholly when you are only its slave.

Italo Calvino, *Invisible Cities*.

Contents

Preface   ix

Introduction   1

1 Inventing scarcity   7

2 The promise of abundance   35

3 Economizing   67

4 Consuming   85

Conclusion   115

Index   119

Preface

The subject of this book might be described in the form of a paradox: why is it that the concept of scarcity as a fundamental aspect of the human condition was born in the relatively affluent societies of the modern west? The answer that I propose is that the presumption of a universal scarcity is a consequence of certain attributes of modernity: of the importance of material objects as signs of relative social status; of the fluidity of status itself; of the effects of commercialization on individual choice. These and other factors combine to create an environment of desire that is necessarily unfulfilled. It is this environment that leads us to experience scarcity as an ever-present condition of our existence.

The writing of this book was undertaken with the assistance of a fellowship from the American Council of Learned Societies and the National Endowment for the Humanities, whose generosity I gratefully acknowledge. Glen Gordon, Lewis Mainzer, George Sulzner and the rest of my colleagues in the department of political science at the University of Massachusetts granted me leave from my teaching responsibilities and supported me in many other, less obvious ways. I am indebted to my former colleagues, William Connolly and Jean Bethke Elshtain, for all that they have done to give me the opportunity to write this book.

During the time I have been thinking about and struggling with this project I have had the singular good fortune to have known Sheldon S. Wolin as a teacher, colleague, and friend. His criticisms and those of Arno J. Mayer on an earlier version of this study convinced me to rethink fundamental aspects of it and have resulted in this very different essay. I cannot hope to have met their exacting standards, but do hope that they will find the effort to have been nonetheless worthwhile. Joyce Appleby's enthusiasm for this project has been a constant source of encouragement to me, as has been the editorial support of Nancy Marten. I am grateful to James Der Derian and Kiaran Honderich for their numerous suggestions and wonderful conviviality during much of the writing. I was able to explore some of the material contained in this book in my graduate seminar and I am indebted to the members of it for many helpful ideas and arguments. Jeneen Hobby's insightful reading of the first chapter helped me enormously in writing the later sections. Lynn Peterfreund's careful criticisms of the entire text (this sentence not withstanding) were, as always, of the greatest importance to me. Finally, while making my way through this depiction of a social world without limits, I enjoyed the unlimited love and selfless generosity of my families, nuclear and extended.

Leverett, Mass.
September, 1988

Introduction

The daily evidence seems incontrovertible, even to those of us who live in apparent comfort. Televised and printed images of poverty and famine are constant reminders of the precariousness of the human condition, justifying Jean-Paul Sartre's confident assertion that "the whole of human development, at least up to now, has been a bitter struggle against *scarcity*."[1] We are accustomed to turning these discrete images into generalized observations of this sort. When we see a picture depicting hunger in the Third World or the American inner city we may attribute it at one level to a specific cause: to a bad harvest or a decline in commodity prices; to government policies or to inherent laziness; to ecological damage or the effects of war. But at the same time we see this picture against a backdrop of experiences from our decently fed daily lives: with the latest audio or video equipment we want but cannot afford; with the long lines of cars endured during a gasoline shortage; with the time we wished we had to do something we enjoy doing. The result is that we see the picture not only as depicting the experience of a particular people in particular circumstances, but also as expressive of something general: of scarcity.

The perception of a general condition of insufficiency is refracted through a prism of choices. Because we experience the necessity of choosing between alternatives, we see an affinity between the absolute neediness of someone experiencing hunger and the relative neediness of someone who cannot have all his or her wants supplied simultaneously. If we sometimes speak of having attained a level of affluence, it is because we think that we have moved from absolute to relative need, but the paradox of this affluence is that it entangles us

in an ever-growing web of choices. We see unmet needs among the
affluent and unmet needs among the impoverished, and so we see the
sense of Lionel Robbins' formulation of the universal problem of the
human species:

> We have been turned out of Paradise. We have neither eternal life
> nor unlimited means of gratification. Everywhere we turn, if we
> choose one thing we must relinquish others which, in different
> circumstances, we would not wish to have relinquished. Scarcity
> of means to satisfy given ends is an almost ubiquitous condition of
> human behavior. Here, then, is the unity of the subject of
> Economic Science, the forms assumed by human behavior in
> disposing of scarce means.[2]

This simple articulation of the so-called scarcity postulate – the
presupposition of scarcity that underlies modern economic theory
and upon which its claim to universality rests – resonates with our
quotidian experience. And so we turn the gaze of the economist that
lives within each of us outward toward the world and backward
toward history and we assume that we understand something
timeless about the human lot.

We assume too much. There is good reason to believe that the
perception of scarcity as a universal condition of the human species,
with all the attendant consequences for behavior such a condition can
be said to entail, is peculiar to the modern Anglo-European eye. The
uncomprehending gaze returned by the "primitive" is one such
reason to doubt the supposed ubiquity of insufficiency. Looking at
some of the world's poorest people, hunters and gatherers, we expect
to find them engaged in a ceaseless pursuit of necessities and
conscious of the precariousness of their situation. But hunters display
few of the characteristics that the scarcity postulate would lead us to
anticipate. Marshall Sahlins, summing up the findings of ethnograph-
ies of native Australians, argues that:

> a good case can be made that hunters and gatherers work less time
> than we do; and, rather than a continuous travail, the food quest is
> intermittent, leisure abundant, and there is a greater amount of
> sleep in the daytime per capita per year than in any other condition
> of society.[3]

Difficult to construe through the glare of the scarcity postulate, the
source of this "affluent" behavior amid absolute poverty is clearly
seen once we shield it from our eyes: the hunters have very few

needs, and those that they have are satisfied with relative ease. This is why Sahlins describes them as "The original affluent society."

Paradoxically, the hunting and gathering societies that are marginal curiosities of the modern world can help to lead us to an understanding of just how curious is the assumption of universal scarcity in the history of the west. When native Australians experience an insufficiency of easily obtainable food, they experience it as an episode, not as a general condition.[4] The etymology of the English word "scarcity" reveals a similar disposition. Of medieval origin, "scarcity" derives from the Old Northern French *escarceté*. Its original usage denoted an insufficiency of supply, and by the fifteenth century the word took on a more specific meaning as an insufficiency of supply of necessities, or dearth. At the same time, the term acquired a clear temporal characteristic signifying a *period* of insufficiency, or *a* dearth. This remained the principal usage until the late nineteenth century, when neoclassical economics made the scarcity postulate its foundation and the term passed into general usage through its transformation into a concept signifying a general condition: not "a scarcity of," or "a time of scarcity," but simply "scarcity."[5] This etymology suggests a history that is discontinuous; that scarcity in the general sense is a modern invention.

Before there was scarcity there were scarci*ties*. Very few conclusions of a general nature followed from the experience of episodes of insufficiency. What thinking was done about this experience was largely Greek in origin. The ancient Greek word *spanis* corresponds to the premodern, limited sense of scarcity, signifying "*scarcity, rareness, dearth, lack of* a thing."[6] This term's meaning is consistent with Greek attitudes toward necessity and needs, which are framed within bounds established by nature and justice. Whether the source is Hesiod's *Works and Days*, dating from around 700 B.C., or Aristotle's *Politics*, written some three centuries later, the idea of insufficiency is determined by a concept of needs as naturally limited. The self-sufficiency of the household and of the polis is a requirement of justice – natural needs can and must be met, where the means to satisfy them are lacking there is *spanis* – but unnatural wants are a threat to a well-balanced soul or a well-balanced community because they are by definition limitless. Hence the persistent concern in Greek texts with *hubris*, with the boundless desire that unbalances an individual and poses a threat to the polis. In one form or another, this general attitude prevailed in western thinking about needs and their satisfactions until the modern era. As long as needs could be interpreted as naturally fixed, their satisfaction only episodically interrupted by a bad harvest or an unplanned mishap, scarcity could retain its limited sense.

In seventeenth-century England, Thomas Hobbes observed that "by desire, we always signify the absence of the object."[7] We may need something that we already possess, but we cannot be said to desire it. If desire is felt, it is because of a lack. Hobbes speculated that we are all desiring beings and that therefore we are in continual motion, ever unsatisfied as we perpetually seek what we do not have. Because human beings occupy a finite world, the motion caused by desire would inevitably cause us to bump into each other, leading to competition, distrust, and fear of untimely death. He saw that if this is the case, there can be only two ways to get ourselves under control. One is death itself, which brings desire to a halt. The other is to repress ourselves; to recognize the threat that our desires pose to each other and to call a truce, guaranteed by a sovereign power authorized for the purpose, that will force us to channel our desires in nonbelligerent directions. This second solution amounts to an institutionalized hubris and Hobbes recognized the degree to which he was transgressing the bounds of the inherited Greek wisdom in putting it forth. He asked his readers to look at themselves rather than to the books containing the inherited wisdom and to see if desire was not the motivator of their actions. Once they admitted that it was – or once they allowed him to convince them that it was – they would accept the necessity of the state's disciplinary power.

Hobbes' contemporaries were reluctant to accept his challenge but in subsequent centuries the desire he so profoundly understood has come to be incorporated into the modern conception of need. We have abandoned the substance of the notion of fixed, natural needs. We continue to speak in terms of basic human needs or subsistence needs, but when we do this it is with the acknowledgment that there is a degree of relativity involved; that needs are really socially specific. When we say that food, clothing, and shelter are basic needs, we usually have some sense of decency in mind, some sense of a standard, either one that we take for granted because it is our own, or one that we attribute to others as their standard. We know full well that different societies and cultures meet these basic needs in radically different ways, so that what is understood to be subsistance from within one culture appears as luxury or penury to another. More difficult still, we cannot agree, either among ourselves or between cultures, on everything that counts as a need beyond the physical requirements of human survival.[8] Is there a human need for privacy? The answer will likely be different in Tokyo than in Manhattan's Upper West Side.

Once a degree of relativity is allowed, the distinction between needs and desires becomes difficult to maintain. This is particularly so if we accept the full ramifications of the notion that material needs are socially constituted. Material goods never simply exist; they are situated within structures of meaning.[9] They mediate social relationships and in doing so become expressive of needs that have their origin in those relationships. Among the social needs constitutive of modern, commercial societies are those of recognition and prestige, and even if some of them run up against absolute limits to their satisfaction,[10] others, particularly those tied to fashion, are capable of apparently infinite expansion. Thus the boundlessness of desire is realized in the proliferation of social needs. For us, the denizens of this world of desire, it is no longer a question of episodic insufficiency: out of our affluence we have created a social world of scarcity.

*

The following chapters will describe how the translation of needs into desires and desires into needs has been effected in social practices and understood by social theorists of various persuasions over the past 250 years. The first chapter is an interpretation of the concept of scarcity as it emerges from the eighteenth-century writings of Adam Smith, David Hume, and, as critique, Jean-Jacques Rousseau. Its correlate, the concept of abundance, is discussed in chapter 2 via such nineteenth-century authors as Thomas Malthus, John Stuart Mill, Karl Marx, and John Ruskin. The third chapter is devoted to an examination of the scarcity postulate as formulated by marginal utility economics later in the century and of the economizing rationality that issues from it. I then turn, in the fourth chapter, to the nature and character of consumption in modernity, taking nineteenth-century Paris as my starting point. My aim is to present a mosaic of interpretation – of texts and practices – out of which a picture will emerge of scarcity and modernity.

NOTES

1 Jean-Paul Sartre, *Critique of Dialectical Reason*, ed. Jonathan Ree, trans. Alan Sheridan-Smith (London: N.L.B. 1976), 23.
2 Lionel Robbins, *The Nature and Significance of Economic Science* (London: Macmillan, 1932), 15.
3 Marshall Sahlins, *Stone Age Economics* (Chicago: Aldine, 1972), 14.
4 Sahlins, *Stone Age Economics*, 30-1.
5 *O.E.D.*
6 Liddell and Scott, *Greek–English Lexicon*.
7 Thomas Hobbes, *Leviathan, or the Matter, Forme and Power of a Commonwealth, Ecclesiasticall and Civil*, ed. Michael Oakeshott (Oxford: Basil Blackwell, 1955), 32.
8 One notable excursion into this area is Michael Ignatieff, *The Needs of Strangers: An Essay on Privacy, Solidarity, and the Politics of Being Human* (New York: Viking, Elisabeth Sifton Books, 1985).
9 See Marshall Sahlins, *Culture and Practical Reason* (Chicago: University of Chicago Press, 1978), chap. 5.
10 This is the case with so-called positional goods such as education at elite universities and bucolic country houses. See Fred Hirsch, *Social Limits to Growth*, A Twentieth Century Fund Study (Cambridge, Mass.: Harvard University Press, 1976).

1

Inventing scarcity

The European eighteenth century saw the invention of the steam engine, the jigsaw puzzle, and the toothpick. It also witnessed the invention of scarcity. The materials that were employed in the construction of this phenomenon had been at hand since the Greeks, but the moderns refashioned these materials into something new. The relationship between needs and desires – indeed, the very definitions of these things – was at the heart of the new conception, but so were thoughts and observations on the human propensity for emulation and the pleasure of gaining recognition, on the workings of envy and invidious distinction. A few writers, Rousseau foremost among them, saw this invention for what it was, but most believed instead that they had made a discovery, revealing what had previously been shrouded in false conceptions influenced by muddled moral notions that could now be discarded as the mystifications they were. It was, after all, the period we call the Age of Enlightenment.

The quotidian experience of these writers was shaped not only by the concepts with which they sought to make sense of it, but also by long-term and large-scale transformations in social life affecting European civilization – the great commercial expansion of the seventeenth and eighteenth centuries, the democratization of politics conveniently symbolized in the English, American, and French Revolutions, and the less easily conceptualized but perhaps equally tangible fluidity of status and class that accompanied commerce and politics. These transformations were particularly acute in northern Europe, were especially obvious in the capital cities, and were most concentrated in London. If, in Walter Benjamin's phrase, Paris can be said to be the capital of the nineteenth century, London is most surely the capital of the eighteenth.

Dr. Johnson's London presents a microcosm of the conditions that gave rise to the invention of scarcity, and it was in London, or while under the influence of it, that the first systematic theory of scarcity was developed. Eighteenth-century London was a central location of the so-called Industrial Revolution then underway, but more importantly it was also a central location – perhaps *the* central location – of a related transformation in consumption, a transformation one historian has termed a "Consumer Revolution."[1] Alongside the evolution of high-volume, standardized production there emerged a pattern of high-volume, standardized consumption driven by the social imperatives of fashion. London combined many characteristics that aided its emergence as a hotbed of fashion. As a capital city, it shared with other capitals the showy ostentation of court life, but to a degree unlike any other capital, this ostentation was close to home. Within easy distance of much of the country, London was a common destination or transit point for a disproportionately high percentage of the English population, 11 per cent of which lived in London in 1750 (up from an already imposing 7 per cent a century earlier), a much higher figure than that for any other European capital. And it is estimated that as much as 16 per cent of the adult population of eighteenth-century England lived in London at some point in their lives.[2] Undoubtedly, much of this population movement resulted from the Enclosures and consisted of people whose margin of existence was slight. But along with these perhaps unwilling London immigrants came many of the people who had set them on the move in the first place. From the point of view of consumption, the establishment of London residences by the country gentry is particularly important, since this upwardly mobile stratum was especially prone to emulative consumption and conspicuous display as it sought to ape the style of the higher nobility just as it was acquiring their country estates.[3] And the gentry's seasonal migration between their newly built Georgian town houses and country homes provided one of the principal mechanisms for the spread of fashion outward from London, enhancing the capital's stature as a trend-setting focal point while spreading the experience and expectation of frequent changes in fashion and taste to the hinterland. Not only did the gentry return from London each spring sporting the latest styles and transporting the latest luxury items, their servants returned with less expensive imitations of these fashionable goods, thus spreading them downward in the social order as well as outward in the spatial order.[4]

This spreading effect was not unintended. By the eighteenth century, entrepreneurs had discovered what economic theory calls the elasticity of demand.[5] Masters of salesmanship were now poised to exploit the idea that domestic markets could be expanded by stimulating the desire for new things and by the introduction of refinement, variety and fashion into objects of everyday use. The desire for new things took several forms: like the late seventeenth- and early eighteenth-century craze for cheap Indian cotton, it could be both instigator and consequence of increased trade; it could be tempted by the introduction of new products of utility, adornment, or amusement; or it could arise from the gradual seepage downward of luxury items as they descended in social class and declined in exclusivity. In this last case, the items were not, strictly speaking, new, but were previously unavailable to many people who could now acquire them. These things were functionally new, and they encompassed everything from tea to children's books.[6]

The stimulation of demand for common items such as clothes and pottery was partly bound up with trade as well, since such demand might be provoked by the importation of foreign fabrics or patterns, or materials such as porcelain. The seventeenth century had seen an expansion of demand along these lines, though the scale was relatively small, such items remaining the province of the wealthy, and therefore categorized as luxuries, until late in the century.[7] But what sets the eighteenth century apart is the purposive role ascribed to fashion and social emulation in the creation of demand for clothes and household goods. Advertisements in local papers placed by merchants recently returned from the capital and the establishment of permanent shops in towns outside London purporting to carry the latest styles abetted the seasonal flow of gentry retinues and increasingly placed high fashion within the grasp of the countryside. Entrepreneurs such as pottery baron Josiah Wedgwood and button magnate Matthew Boulton seized on the potential for emulative buying and made a point of currying favor with London's fashionable set and foreign aristocrats in order to sell in great quantities to the general public. Boulton held his annual show, complete with special, private viewings for the trend-setters, at Easter, which marked the end of the London season, thus ensuring that his buttons would be treated as up-to-the-minute when the gentry returned to their estates, stimulating an emulative demand for them.[8] Wedgwood made it a policy to keep his initial prices high on new designs in order to enhance the snob appeal of his goods, reasoning that "a great price is at first necessary to make the vases esteemed *Ornaments for Palaces*."[9] Once a design was well established in this estimation, he would put it into mass production, only then dropping the price, while simultaneously introducing a new design to the fashionable. Thus would begin another cycle of prestige consumption and emulative buying.[10]

The techniques and innovations employed by Boulton, Wedgwood, and their contemporaries to exploit the new-found elasticity of demand thus helped to solidify the expectation of changing fashion, of frequent if sometimes subtle shifts in taste and style. An environment was thereby created in which people were increasingly confronted by things they desired but did not have. The spreading of commercial relations through English society, symbolized most clearly in the Enclosures and their effects, established money as the mediator of desire, helping to fix it upon things that could be purchased, particularly upon the vastly expanding world of fashionable things. Because these things had a price, all that was needed to possess them was money – not family name or breeding – and so they were at least theoretically within reach, making them possible objects of desire. The thinking that was done about needs was adjusted accordingly. Needs that are conceived to be naturally based, such as needs for food, shelter, sex, etc., can be approached discretely. That is, the need for food can be met, or not met, independently of the need for shelter. This is consistent with the notion of discrete scarcities discussed in the previous chapter. But when these needs become intertwined with a fluid, ever-changing social world of emulation and conspicuous consumption, they become transformed into an indiscrete desire constantly shifting its focus from one unpossessed object to another. Thus while seventeenth-century writers, preoccupied by a series of poor harvests, could still concern themselves with cyclical scarcities, their eighteenth-century counterparts moved in a world of dramatically increased excitation and frustration of desire, and therefore in a world of perpetual scarcity.[11]

*

The dynamics of such a world were well understood by two of the greatest intellects of the age, and the two central figures of the so-called Scottish Enlightenment, David Hume and Adam Smith. Though Smith's language in his *Lectures on Jurisprudence* is one that employs concepts of necessity and taste rather than need and desire, his analysis is consistent with the notion that by the eighteenth century it was possible to see no significant difference between human needs and desires. Smith argues that the human being, unlike other animals, is not content with what is given in nature for the satisfaction of needs, since the human being is governed in part by taste – by a preference for beauty and variety. It is thus the case, he observes, that

> the whole industry of human life is employed not in procuring the supply of our three humble necessities, food, cloaths, and lodging, but in procuring the conveniences of it according to the nicety and delicacey of our taste. To improve and multiply the materials which are the principal objects of our necessities, gives occasion to all the variety of the arts.[12]

Such a view of the restlessness of human desire had been expressed earlier, in the 1690s, in the context of debates over the consumption of imported luxury goods.[13] But Smith and his Scottish contemporaries built an elaborate theory of "civil society" upon it, a theory which discerned the movement of history in the refinement of taste.

A key element in the view of civil society that frames the reflections of Smith and Hume is the functional role attributed to the concept of luxury. While some Scottish Enlightenment writers, such as Adam Ferguson, continued an older tradition of associating luxury with corruption,[14] Smith and Hume saw that once need and desire become conceptually indistinguishable, it becomes equally difficult to separate, morally or conceptually, needs and luxuries – the movement of desire ensures that old luxuries will become new needs as desire, ever dissatisfied, shifts its focus to new luxuries. Feeding desire with new luxuries helps to move humanity along a trajectory defined by the refinement of taste and the development of new needs. "And this perhaps is the chief advantage which arises from a commerce with strangers," Hume claims. "It rouses men from their indolence; and presenting the gayer and more opulent part of the nation with objects of luxury, which they never before dreamed of, raises in them a desire of a more splendid way of life than what their ancestors enjoyed."[15] Once exposed to new objects of desire, Hume goes on to argue, the demand thus stimulated will encourage the imitation of imported luxuries by domestic manufacturers, and encourage as well the likes of Boulton and Wedgwood

> towards some refinement in other commodities, which may be wanted at home. And there must always be materials for them to work upon; till every person in the state, who possesses riches, enjoys as great plenty of home commodities, and those in as great perfection, as he desires; which can never possibly happen.[16]

It can never happen because the insatiable quality of desire ensures that demand is infinitely elastic.

Hume's reflections on the benefits of trade are consistent with his friend Adam Smith's formulation of the concept of wealth as "the produce of the land and labour of . . . society," understanding that produce to include "all the necessaries and conveniences of life."[17] Given the views they shared on the inherent impulse toward refinement of taste, they could not with any consistency maintain a functional distinction between necessary and superfluous goods. All goods must count as wealth. So, by Hume's reasoning, trade, by introducing new things as luxuries, stimulates emulative desire, which in turn stimulates the creation of wealth. The creation of wealth, in turn, is a measure of the degree of refinement achieved by a society – the wealthiest societies will be the most refined because they will have provided the greatest range for the exercise of desire. This is one of the reasons why Hume argued for the superiority of modern over ancient society: the spread of commerce among the moderns had expanded the arts and given greater range to human potential.[18] The evidence would have been apparent to Hume and Smith, and to many of their readers, as they moved through the crowded streets of London, past the glittering shop windows, an innovation of the eighteenth century developed to display, and thus to help create, the new wealth.[19]

While this conception of wealth is based on a theory of taste as a natural human attribute, it clearly contains as well a social dimension, as can be seen in Hume's assertion that desire must be stimulated by some external means in order to rouse it from a lethargic acceptance of the status quo and spur it on to "a more splendid way of life." The human being may have an innate sense of refinement through which to mediate his or her needs, but left to oneself, that innate sense would languish. We are not left to ourselves, however, and Hume and Smith both emphasize the roles of emulation and recognition as central features of desire – features that go beyond the consequences of the introduction of foreign luxury goods alone to account for the dynamics of modern society in general.

Arguments over the benefits and evils of luxury were commonplace in eighteenth-century Britain as writers and moral theorists tried to come to terms with the new commercial expansion. Not surprisingly, a great many words were spent in denouncing the effects of envy and conspicuous consumption, often in the context of denouncing (or, less often, in defending) Bernard Mandeville's satiric *The Fable of the Bees: or, Private Vices, Publick Benefits*.[20] In their contributions to this literature Hume and Smith do not denounce, but they applaud with only one hand apiece. For his part, Hume set himself the task of trying to understand what he takes as a given; namely, why it is that "nothing has a greater tendency to give us an esteem for any person, than his power and riches; or a contempt, than his poverty and meanness."[21] His conclusion centers on the notion of sympathy, which is a staple of the Scottish moral philosophy of the time. We all enjoy the sight of beautiful houses, gardens, carriages, etc., Hume reasons, because the sight of beautiful things gives us pleasure. But we go beyond that to connect the things we see to the person who possesses them, a person who, however distant from us in status and wealth (and the wealth we see signifies the status) is nevertheless a person, and so we are able to imagine ourselves in his or her position *vis-à-vis* those things. In the eighteenth-century language, we sympathize with that person. But sympathy in this sense works both ways, and so Hume notes that the possessors of wealth gain an additional pleasure out of the esteem they know they are commanding from us. Further, we know that they know it and that they are gaining pleasure from that knowledge, and so a spiral of vicarious pleasure emanates from the objects of wealth.[22] Situated at the center of that spiral, the possessors of wealth get a double satisfaction: not only do they get the direct pleasures that riches afford, they also get the indirect pleasure that comes from the regard of others. This is what Hume emphasizes in summing up his conclusions on the matter:

> There is certainly an original satisfaction in riches deriv'd from that power, which they bestow, of enjoying all the pleasures of life; and as this is their very nature and essence, it must be the first

source of all the passions, which arise from them. One of the most considerable of these passions is that of love or esteem in others, which therefore proceeds from a sympathy with the pleasure of the possessor. But the possessor has also a secondary satisfaction in riches arising from the love and esteem he acquires by them, and this satisfaction is nothing but a second reflexion of that original pleasure, which proceeded from himself. This secondary satisfaction or vanity becomes one of the principal recommendations of riches, and is the chief reason, why we either desire them for ourselves, or esteem them in others.[23]

So Hume's treatment softens the problem of envy, formulating it as a question of esteem, but in doing this he also places the interpretation of wealth and the motivations associated with it squarely in the area of social relations, where the analysis of desire and luxury had led him, rather than in the area of human nature.[24]

Smith's discussion of wealth and esteem is consistent with Hume's, but harder edged in its assessments, and he begins with a paradox. In *The Theory of Moral Sentiments*, Smith points out a truth about the luxuries of wealth that seems obvious: that if we approach wealth from the perspective of old age or sickness,

> power and riches appear then to be, what they are, enormous and operose [laborious] machines contrived to produce a few trifling conveniences to the body. . . . They keep off the summer shower, not the winter storm, but leave [their possessor] always as much, and sometimes more exposed than before, to anxiety, to fear, and to sorrow; to diseases, to danger and to death.[25]

Why, then, do people relentlessly pursue wealth and luxury? The answer Smith offers is that we do not normally, of course, see wealth from the afflicted condition of the sick-bed or from the retrospective point of view of the death-bed; we see it instead from the standpoint of a "spectator," a hypothetical Other embodying the values and customs of a given society. From this contemporaneous point of view, and once again employing the tool of sympathy, it is easy enough to see the satisfactions afforded by the homes and gardens of the wealthy, satisfactions which Smith, unlike Hume, ascribes to "conveniency" and "utility" rather than to the more ephemeral pleasures of beauty.[26] More difficult to explain are frivolous examples of fashionable luxuries, such as "the curiosity of a toothpick, or an ear-picker, of a machine for cutting the nails, or of any other trinket of the same kind."[27] But these frivolities, too, carry with them the appearance of comfort and convenience; they are seen not so much as the stuff of happiness as they are "means of happiness," though not such unambiguously appealing means as houses and gardens. These latter, therefore, "more effectually gratify that love of distinction so natural to man."[28] However, this recourse to natural impulses should be placed in the context of the knowledge that a significant growth in the organized viewing of art collections in country houses occurred in the eighteenth century,[29] a practice that would have had the effect of showing off the houses, their luxurious contents, and the gardens surrounding them along with the Old Masters. Signs of distinction, all.

Though Smith disparages the thought that the happiness material wealth makes possible is anything more than an illusion, the illusion itself plays an important role in his understanding of the production of wealth. He observes that

> the pleasures of wealth and greatness . . . strike the imagination as something grand and beautiful and noble, of which the attainment is well worth all the toil and anxiety which we are so apt to bestow upon it, [adding that] it is well that nature imposes upon us in this manner. It is this deception which rouses and keeps in continual motion the industry of mankind.[30]

The knowledge that true happiness does not lie in the possession of material things might lead to a society devoted to contemplation or art, but it would be a society poor in wealth. Thankfully, from this standpoint, we live under the illusion of material happiness, and so the playing out of social emulation – the pursuit of social distinction through material things – leads us to produce those "necessaries and conveniences of life" by which Smith defined wealth. But while the things themselves will not bring happiness, their acquisition and display do bring a kind of "secondary satisfaction," as Hume put it, a second order happiness that results from the esteem of others. "The rich man," Smith writes

> glories in his riches, because he feels that they naturally draw upon him the attention of the world. . . . At the thought of this, his heart seems to swell and dilate itself within him, and he is fonder of his wealth, upon this account, than for all the other advantages it procures him.[31]

So the functional advantages of emulative desire at least carry the reward, for the successful competitors, of the regard of others – whether we call it envy or esteem, no matter.

It is obvious that a system of emulative competition such as the one described by Hume and Smith presupposes a context of material inequality, otherwise there would be no have-nots to esteem the haves, but it must be an inequality of a particular kind. Historians of the eighteenth-century English commercial revolution, often citing as evidence the journals and reports of contemporary travelers to England, emphasize the relatively egalitarian nature of social relations that prevailed, with a short leap from one class, or rank, to another.[32] Some sense of the possibility of rising up the social ladder is indeed necessary if people are to conceive of emulating those above in order to get to where they are. Smith noted something of this sort when he argued that the trickle down effect of luxury is dependent on "a graduall declension and subordinate degrees of wealth."[33] But he noted, too, that such an arrangement for the realization of the rewards of prosperity requires as well the looming punishment of the law in order to "hinder the poor from ever acquiring the wealth by violence which they would otherwise exert on the rich; they tell them they must either continue poor or acquire wealth in the same manner as they have done."[34] As the barriers between ranks become more porous, the integrity of the system regulating passage between them must be clearly maintained – in this kind of situation, tradition will not do.

Tradition was sufficient as long as the social order was one defined exclusively by birth. Then, the barriers between ranks were impenetrable and, equally important, the signs of one rank were out of bounds to any other. A serf could not aspire to be a lord, of course, but neither could a merchant or tradesman; nor could they aspire to the lifestyle that was the lord's prerogative – there could be no emulative competition between ranks. Where the competition was centered was within ranks, particularly among the late feudal aristocracy, where a count would relentlessly try to outdo another count, but where none but a duke would attempt to display the lifestyle of a duke; to do otherwise would be to invite ridicule and social death among the only society that mattered to them, the court society that was possessed of the taste necessary to distinguish between the outward appearances of count and duke.[35] In the world of court society, there was deemed to be a lifestyle appropriate to each rank of the nobility; the lifestyle could be read as a sign of the rank by anyone who could decipher the courtly sign-system. It was imperative not only that each noble should avoid poaching on the lifestyle of another rank, but that they maintain their own, even if it should mean economic ruin. The wealth displayed signified rank. So a noble's rank determined the degree of prestige display that was appropriate, and in this manner it makes sense to say that the system of aristocratic ranks served as a limit on such display, even though prestige was the central concern of this society.

By the eighteenth century in England, emulative competition had escaped the restricted society of the court and had spread to the provincial gentry and the middle class. Birth and wealth, though still mostly connected in practice, were no longer directly expressive of each other – there were ruined gentry selling their houses to rich merchants. Adam Smith still connects them in a comment in which he recognizes that the society of emulative competition he has described requires that wealth stand alone as the object of desire and the mark of authority:

> Nature has wisely judged that the distinction of ranks, the peace and order of society, would rest more securely upon the plain and palpable difference of birth and fortune, than upon the invisible and uncertain difference of wisdom and virtue. The undistinguishing eye of the great mob of mankind can well enough perceive the former: it is with difficulty that the nice discernment of the wise and virtuous can sometimes distinguish the latter.[36]

But as birth becomes less immediately expressive of wealth, and therefore less easily discernable, the sign of wealth becomes preeminent among "the undistinguishing eye of the great mob of mankind." The fine distinctions that govern the etiquette of court society must give way to a vulgar appreciation of wealth as a conspicuous display anyone can read.[37] Further, fashion, though it may originate in court circles, must increasingly become universal in its appeal, slicing downward through ranks. Over the course of the eighteenth century, for example, the clothing of the rich became less extreme in style and more nuanced with respect to material and cut, thus satisfying both the desire of the fashionable to stand out, and of the middle class to emulate them, as best they could.[38]

As the distances separating the ranks narrow, so too do differences in style, but then the small distinctions that remain become extremely important in defining social status and prestige. No longer tied to a more or less fixed order of social ranks, wealth ceases to signify anything other than itself. To put it another way, one's status no longer dictates one's lifestyle; the display of wealth now signifies wealth, and therefore status, relative to other displays of wealth. Smith's "spectator" is, in effect, the judge in this game of status recognition, a judge who stands within the boundaries of the game. The spectator does not represent an external order or set of principles that determine the status of the players. Instead, the spectator, the Other who embodies the judgments internal to the social game of emulative competition, is a mediator intervening between two players and establishing the status relationship between them. It is by recourse to this hypothetical Other that one is able to stand outside oneself and view one's own position *vis-à-vis* another's: it is a process of social triangulation, a means of measuring relative esteem.

Hume holds out the possibility that the same love of esteem that leads us to desire riches will also lead us to desire a good reputation, and that this second desire will place some limits upon the first, but Smith's theory of the triangular structure of social recognition reveals the futility that lies behind his friend's hope. As we have seen, Hume's reflections on esteem are framed within a two-sided relationship of Self and Other – what Hume depicts as a mirror-like process of reflection.[39] He argues that we value more highly the esteem of those who are closer to us than of those who are distant, and of those whom we esteem more than of those whom we consider fools. Conversely, we feel a sharper sting of rejection if we lack the esteem of family, friends, or those we admire than we feel from the disregard of strangers or fools.[40] So we are mostly concerned with the approbation of those who are most like us and who reflect our own sense of ourselves. Hume thus sees people operating within social circles, defining themselves in the terms appropriate to them, and adopting appropriate styles of behavior in order to maintain a good reputation within them. Sympathy may enable us to esteem the rich from a distance, but the emulative effect upon us will be weaker than the desire to secure the esteem of those near to us. In this case, emulative competition would indeed be limited, taking place in a predominantly horizontal plane and confined to a criterion of appropriateness determined within each of the different levels of social stratification.

While there is undeniably much sense to this depiction of daily social life, it jars against Hume's own interpretation of emulation in his analysis of luxury and the progress of refinement. There, as we have seen, it is the introduction of an object (or objects) from some external source that is the stimulator of desire and the spur to emulation. This pattern, which Hume claims then gets repeated internally, suggests a process of vertical emulation. Such a process can only be possible if there is a language, a sign system, that can be read in roughly the same way throughout the society, overriding the subsystems that govern social circles. Smith's notion of the spectator is recognition of such a sign system, since the hypothetical Other embodies a general social sense, not that of a particular circle. Instead of Hume's bipolar, horizontal distinction between Self and Other, Smith's triangular formulation suggests a vertical relationship constituted by the Self, the object of comparison (which is a subject), and the Other (the spectator). In this relationship, the Self is able to transcend its own social circle and make comparisons with those above or below in the social order.[41] Smith's version of the bases of emulation thus seems to make better sense of Hume's observations on luxury than does Hume's own focus on family and friends.

It has been claimed that Hume's own social circle, "the fashionable world of the nobility and the gentry, revolving around the club, the coffee-house, the salon, and the country estate," forms the context for properly understanding his notion of reputation and the limits it places upon acquisitiveness.[42] But recourse to Hume's social milieu also serves to underline the competitive stakes involved in the scramble for social status, since the position of the nobility and gentry was not fixed but was something that had to be constantly maintained. This was indeed a "fashionable" world; as we have already seen, Hume's milieu was at the center of the selling strategies of the new entrepreneurs, a strategy that was dependent upon the dynamic of prestige consumption so important to a gentry eager to mimic the lifestyle of the higher nobility, and to a middle class eager to mimic the gentry.[43] Such a world necessitates a constant scrambling after the latest luxuries in order to keep up and to keep in front. Acquisitiveness is thus built into the desire merely to maintain one's social standing: the comparative triangle is employed to gauge the distance behind as well as the distance ahead. The gentry, at the center of the period's social flux, would have been particularly sensitive to the relentlessness of the struggle, a relentlessness described more than a century later in the following terms by

Thorstein Veblen in *The Theory of the Leisure Class* (1899):

> So soon as the possession of property becomes the basis of popular
> esteem . . . it becomes also a requisite to that complacency which
> we call self-respect. In any community where goods are held in
> severalty it is necessary, in order to his own peace of mind, that an
> individual should possess as large a portion of goods as others with
> whom he is accustomed to class himself; and it is extremely
> gratifying to possess something more than others. But as fast as a
> person makes new acquisitions, and becomes accustomed to the
> resulting new standard of wealth, the new standard forthwith
> ceases to afford appreciably greater satisfaction than the earlier
> standard did. The tendency in any case is constantly to make the
> present pecuniary standard the point of departure for a fresh
> increase of wealth; and this in turn gives rise to a new standard of
> sufficiency and a new pecuniary classification of one's self
> compared with one's neighbours.[44]

As we have seen, the eighteenth-century social theorists had already
grasped the bases and consequences of this dynamic of emulation and
distinction.[45] It is this dynamic that is expressed in Hume's famous
formulation in the *Treatise of Human Nature* of the place of scarcity
in the foundations of justice. Having established society in order to
overcome through the division of labor the "cruelty" of a nature that
has saddled the human being with "numberless wants and necessities" and "slender means" for dealing with them,[46] the social self
discovers that "his wants multiply every moment upon him" while
"his abilities are still more augmented."[47] Those multiplying wants
are unexplained by Hume; they are simply noted as he proceeds to
explain that the division of labor propels society along, satisfying
these proliferating wants as fast as they are generated. But they can be
easily explained as Hume elsewhere explains them: as the quotidian
experience of fashion, status competition, the desire for social
recognition, and other characteristic elements of a social order
ceaselessly redefining itself through the sign system of wealth.

Hume universalized that experience in the *Treatise* when he used
it to establish a dynamic social scarcity to theoretically balance a
static natural scarcity. Though society expands our creative powers
enormously, there is never quite enough to go around because there is
always some new want around the corner. The harsh, brutal
insufficiencies of the isolated individual are contrasted with the
comfortable wants of refinement and taste that, though also natural,

only society imposes as it makes their emergence possible. Natural scarcity accounts for the origins of society; social scarcity for the origins and necessity of justice, since in such an environment everyone will see the need to ensure the possession of what they have while they set their sights on getting more.[48] By discovering the scarcity that provides the background condition for nature and society, and by placing it at the center of his theory of the origins and utility of justice, Hume, as much as anyone, can lay claim to be the inventor of scarcity.

*

A decade after the publication of Hume's *Treatise*, Jean-Jacques Rousseau, responding to a question posed by the Academy of Dijon, won the Academy's prize with an essay attacking the corrupting influence of progress in the arts and sciences. The essay, the *Discourse on the Sciences and Arts*, launched Rousseau's career as a writer and social theorist, a career that would lead him, in 1766, to London under the care and protection of David Hume. That now infamous episode began promisingly enough, with Hume exclaiming in a letter shortly after their arrival together in London that Rousseau was "very amiable, always polite, gay often, commonly sociable. . . . I love him much, and hope that I have some share in his affections."[49] Six months later, Hume, renowned for his good temper, among other virtues, was writing that Rousseau "is surely the blackest and most atrocious Villain, beyond comparison, that now exists in the World."[50] For his part, Rousseau was sure that Hume was part of a plot to undo him. The meeting of the two great minds had ended badly.

The affair was largely a product of Rousseau's unstable paranoia and Hume's overreaction to it, but in retrospect it is easy to see that a clash was likely, if not inevitable. Temperamentally, the two were worlds apart. The urbane, sceptical Hume was at home in the London intellectual scene, even if he periodically complained about it. Rousseau was constantly at odds with the salon society of Parisian letters, even as he was the darling of it. When he made his move to London, his fame and celebrity status was as much an irritation as a pleasure to him, while his companion Thérèse and his dog were sources of embarrassment to his hosts. Rousseau always made a point of desiring the solitude his gifts as a writer made impossible; he sought the recognition of the salon even as he disdained its comforts.

These differences in personality would be interesting but irrelevant if they did not help to expose a difference in temperament between the attitudes assumed by their respective theories of scarcity. Hume's theory is, as we have seen, one which analyzes the dynamic of social needs and integrates it into a broader theory of progress (under the category of refinement). The scarcity experienced in commercial society is thus seen as necessary and is accordingly treated positively as a given. The same can be said for Smith's perspective, although he more often explicitly assumes the position of someone viewing a system from the outside. Rousseau's theory, in contrast, is a critical theory of social scarcity generated from the perspective of someone who is simultaneously pulled and repelled by the social dynamic under investigation.[51] While Hume and Smith describe the utility of a social order based on the external signs of wealth, Rousseau fulminates against an order based on artifice and the refinement by which it judges itself. The battle is engaged at the very outset, in the *Discourse on the Sciences and Arts*, and marks the main theme of Rousseau's career:

> The mind has its needs, as has the body. The latter make up the foundations of society, the former make for its being agreeable. While the Government and the Laws see to the safety and the well-being of men assembled, the Sciences, Letters, and Arts, less despotic and perhaps more powerful, spread garlands of flowers over the iron chains with which they are laden, throttle in them the sentiment of that original freedom for which they seemed born, make them love their slavery, and fashion them into what is called civilized Peoples. Need raised up Thrones; the Sciences and Arts have made them strong.[52]

This formulation contrasts neatly with Hume's: both view society as founded upon need, but whereas the Scot focuses on the benefits of the new needs generated by society, the Genevan focuses instead on the new dependencies such needs entail. In a footnote to the passage extracted above, Rousseau observes that princes encourage superfluities among their people (so long as they do not cost the prince anything) because "they well know that all the needs which a People imposes on itself are so many chains which it assumes." Citing the example of the "Savages of America" who "have proved impossible to tame," Rousseau concludes: "Indeed, what yoke could be imposed upon men who need nothing?"[53]

Rousseau sees the signs of social slavery in the conventions of civilized life and its symbols of success. Employing a familiar contrast of a declining virtuous rusticity with the corrupt urban manners of advancing civilization, he complains of the resulting opacity and uniformity in social relations; where once it was possible to read a person's character from their conduct, in modern society we can read only wealth and taste, while character is hidden behind conventions of etiquette and propriety.[54] Those conventions, to which Rousseau turned more directly in his *Discourse on the Origin and the Foundations of Inequality among Men* (the so-called *Second Discourse* of 1755), are the result of a desire for recognition and esteem that society induces and that provokes individuals to construct a socially acceptable self. To illustrate his argument, Rousseau has recourse to a literary construction: the so-called noble savage in the state of nature. Rousseau envisions an autarchic individual roaming pristine forests without need of anyone else, easily securing rudimentary requirements of food, shelter, and clothing as they arise, without foresight. Similarly, the natural individual is seen as satisfying the desire for sex as the desire arises; that is, through chance encounters, with no second, or future, thought. In contrast to the image of a naturally restless desire propagated by Smith and Hume, Rousseau concludes that in a natural state desire is limited in character, as yet unprovoked by any ideas that go beyond immediate physical need.[55] The realm of unsatisfied desire is the social realm, where desire is spurred on by, and mediated through, comparison. Even in the most rudimentary society, Rousseau observes:

> everyone began to look at everyone else and to wish to be looked at himself, and public esteem acquired a value. The one who sang or danced best; the handsomest, the strongest, the most skillful, or the most eloquent came to be the most highly regarded.[56]

The desire for recognition becomes a need, one which can never be fully satisfied but which must be constantly renewed, replenished in the coin of socially acceptable qualities. Spurred by the desire for the regard of others in terms of these qualities,

> one soon had to have them or to affect them; for one's own advantage one had to seem other than one in fact was. To be and to appear became two entirely different things, and from this

distinction arose ostentatious display, deceitful cunning, and all the vices that follow in their train. Looked at in another way, man, who had previously been free and independent, is now so to speak subjugated by a multitude of new needs to the whole of Nature, and especially to those of his kind, whose slave he in a sense becomes even by becoming their master. . . . Finally, consuming ambition, the ardent desire to raise one's relative fortune less out of genuine need than in order to place oneself above others, instills in all men a black inclination to harm one another.[57]

Drawing his argument to a close, Rousseau poses the distinction sharply between the authentic self of the natural being and the inauthentic self of the social being: "the Savage lives in himself; sociable man, always outside himself, is capable of living only in the opinion of others and, so to speak, derives the sentiment of his own existence solely from their judgment."[58]

It is clear that while Rousseau tends to set up nature and society as oppositions, it is his contemporary society he has in mind, not society as such.[59] All societies would seem to share the problem of social esteem to some degree, but Rousseau is careful to introduce elements such as private property and the division of labor that intensify the problem and that bring his argument into focus around modern European society. Similarly, Rousseau plays off ancient virtue with modern corruption, indicating that at least some complex societies are able to keep invidious distinction under wraps, unlike his own society. And Rousseau's own rootless existence is emblematic of the social fluidity of modernity. Rousseau's constant preoccupation with self-interrogation, reflected in the titles of his *Confessions* and *Rousseau juge de Jean-Jacques*, are evidence of the depth of his conviction that the Delphic inscription, "know thyself," which he proclaims at the outset of his preface to the *Second Discourse* to be his essential concern, was especially problematic in his own time. When Rousseau looks to see who he is, he discovers a self that does not know what is genuine and what is artificial in its makeup. The modern self cannot be defined by its lineage or its rootedness in a particular place; "Citizen of Geneva," the title Rousseau appropriated for the authorship of the *Second Discourse*, is both true and false (he had long since ceased to live in the city of his birth, from which he departed at age sixteen); it is just one of several identifications Rousseau could have chosen, no one of which would have been, at bottom, any less arbitrary than any other. In modernity,

Rousseau says, we are defined externally, and we can never be certain who we are or that our desires are truly our own. The natural self lurks somewhere beneath the socially constructed self, causing us to question the needs we have adopted from without and providing assurance that once we first question who we are we will never quite be comfortable with ourselves again. But the natural self has become so thoroughly covered over that it can only be revealed by conjecture and never truly known, leaving us with no sure footing for our self-identity. Rousseau's life and writings exemplify the unease that results once the façade of the social self is breached.

If the *Discourses* can be seen collectively as a diagnosis of the predicament of the modern self, Rousseau approaches the possibility of a cure in two works published in 1762: *Emile* and *Social Contract*. The first, half treatise, half novel, details the education of its protagonist, Emile, to virtue in a corrupt society. Knowing that there can be no return to the natural self for someone already under the domination of socially induced desire, Rousseau proposes to educate an individual from birth in order to preserve the senses from their corruption by reason and their distortion by social convention.[60] A recurrent theme is the necessity of restricting needs so as to restrict dependency, allowing the individual to attain self-sufficiency and autonomy amid society. Asserting that happiness consists in a balance between desire and the power to satisfy it, a balance which exists for the natural man, Rousseau argues that the imagination is the source of unhappiness, since "it is imagination which extends for us the measure of the possible . . . and which consequently excites and nourishes the desires by the hope of satisfying them." He continues with what amounts to an indictment of social scarcity:

> But the object which at first appeared to be at hand flees more quickly than it can be pursued. When one believes that one has reached it, it transforms and reveals itself in the distance ahead of us. No longer seeing the country we have already crossed, we count it for nothing; what remains to cross ceaselessly grows and extends. Thus one exhausts oneself without getting to the end, and the more one gains on enjoyment, the further happiness gets from us.
>
> On the contrary, the closer to his natural condition man has stayed, the smaller is the difference between his faculties and his desires, and consequently the less removed he is from being happy. He is never less unhappy than when he appears entirely destitute,

for unhappiness consists not in the privation of things but in the need that is felt for them.[61]

Surveying the scene he has drawn of a miserably relentless pursuit of an elusive desire, Rousseau observes that "the real world has its limits; the imaginary world is infinite. Unable to enlarge the one, let us restrict the other."[62] So at least one possible solution to the problem posed by social emulation, which is a source of imagination, is to devise a form of education, necessarily beginning at birth, that would insulate the individual from its allure.

The *Social Contract* addresses the problem of the self and of social needs not from the point of view of the individual, but from that of the polity. In this text the solution is sought in legislation. A legislator, who stands outside the political order, establishes the laws in such a way as to discourage luxury, maintain a narrow differential between wealth and poverty, and substitute the equalizing comparison of one autonomous *citoyen* with another for the competitive distinctions made by one dependent *bourgeois* with another.

As a republican utopia, such a solution parallels the solution proffered by *Emile*, since the society would be subjected to a kind of political education from birth, with institutions molded toward the purpose of minimizing the effects of emulative competition. Such a society, though not rich, would be one that did not experience scarcity in the way Hume, Smith, and Rousseau understand it to be experienced in the modern world. But to effect this solution in reality rather than in a utopian way – to solve the problem for a fully grown modern society rather than for one being born – would entail authoritarian means, as recourse to a legislator would suggest.[63] It would require the repression of desires already stimulated and the transfiguration of a socially mobile order into one with strict limitations on wealth and its acquisition. It would entail, too, the maintenance by the state of a rigid moral code, a civil religion, with the aim of fostering a regard for the collective over the self. In Rousseau's infamous phrase, such a society would be "forced to be free."

Neither of Rousseau's proposals for eliminating the sources of social scarcity is very attractive: the first because it entails a laborious and probably impossible revolution from below; the second because it necessitates a republic of virtue imposed, initially at least, by a revolution from above. But his conjectures flesh out his analysis of the problem of scarcity in modernity. He repeatedly emphasizes the importance of smallness of scale for a style of life antithetical to the workings of social emulation and accumulative competition. The anonymity of large-scale social organization encourages display as a source of recognition and necessitates a social sign system with a common denominator in order to effect that recognition. Living in a society less commercialized than the London based society of Hume and Smith, Rousseau's ruminations on the effects of commerce in generating such a system are not as nuanced as those of the Scots, but the interpretations of all three merge on this point: in modernity, relative wealth is the principal signifier of distinction, and the quest for wealth, together with the instability attendant upon maintaining social standing by means of it, is the principal source of the quotidian experience of scarcity.

NOTES

1 Neil McKendrick, "Introduction" and "The consumer revolution of eighteenth-century England," in Neil McKendrick, John Brewer, and J.H. Plumb, *The Birth of a Consumer Society: The Commercialization of Eighteenth-Century England* (Bloomington, Ind.: Indiana University Press, 1985).

2 E.A. Wrigley, "A simple model of London's importance in Changing English society and economy, 1650-1750," *Past and Present* 37 (1967): 45-9.

3 On the significance of the gentry in this context, see F.J. Fisher, "The development of London as a centre of conspicuous consumption in the sixteenth and seventeenth centuries," *Transactions of the Royal Historical Society*, 4th series, vol. 30 (1948).

4 McKendrick, "The commercialization of Fashion," in McKendrick, et al., *Birth of a Consumer Society*, 56-60, 74; Eric L. Jones, "The fashion manipulators," in L.P. Cain and P.J. Uselding, eds., *Business Enterprise and Economic Change* (Kent, Ohio: Kent State University Press, 1973), 211.

5 For the seventeenth-century background, largely centered on debates over the balance of trade, see Joyce Appleby, *Economic Thought and Ideology in Seventeenth-Century England* (Princeton: Princeton University Press, 1978), esp. chap. 7. By 1690, a mania for printed Indian cotton, deftly cultivated by the

East India Company, led to a rethinking of the assumptions underlying the relationship between needs and markets:

> A new definition of wealth was in order. When the maverick spirit of fashion revealed itself in the craze over printed calicoes the potential market power of previously unfelt wants came clearly into view. Here was a revolutionary force. Under the sway of new tastes, people had spent more, and in spending more the elasticity of demand had become apparent. In this elasticity, the defenders of domestic spending discovered the propulsive power of envy, emulation, love of luxury, vanity, and vaulting ambition.

Appleby, *Economic Thought and Ideology*, 169.

6   For tea, see McKendrick, "Consumer revolution," in McKendrick, et al., *Birth of a Consumer Society*, 28-9; for children's books, see J.H. Plumb, "The new world of children in eighteenth-century England," in ibid., 306.

7   Jones, "The fashion manipulators," 205-7.

8   McKendrick, "The commercialization of fashion," 74.

9   Quoted in Jones, "The fashion manipulators," 219.

10 Jones, "The fashion manipulators," 219. Wedgwood's marketing acumen is discussed in detail in Neil McKendrick, "Josiah Wedgwood and the commercialization of the Potteries," in McKendrick, et al., *Birth of a Consumer Society*, 100-45.

The basic elements of manipulating fashion have not changed much in the past two centuries. The marketing of so-called designer labels today, complete with discount outlets for suburban trend followers, is merely an elaboration on an old theme. But even more to the point is the comment by the owner of an avant-garde clothing store for the Hollywood fashion set who explains, "We know what they want. . . . Sometimes we get them what they want before they know it. Most people stay a step behind the present. We're trying to stay a step ahead." Quoted in Michael Gross, "Avant-garde styles in a hidden oasis," *New York Times*, September 29, 1987.

11 Joyce Appleby, *Economic Thought and Ideology*, 98, expresses a similar point when she argues that:

> the new scarcity is an abstraction – a hypothetical condition created when people's desires outdistance actual goods. The real scarcity of a subsistence economy with population

pressing upon its productive resources had now been replaced by the psychological scarcities of imagined wants heightened by a commerce rapidly extending in size and diversity of goods.

My argument, however, is that only the "abstract" condition of scarcity is "real."

12 Adam Smith, *Lectures on Jurisprudence*, ed. R.L. Meek, D.D. Raphael, and P.G. Stein (Oxford: Clarendon Press, 1978), 488. The passage excerpted is from the lectures of 1766.

13 Nicholas Barbon had made the point emphatically in his treatise, *A Discourse of Trade*, when he argued that:

> The Wants of the Mind are infinite, Man naturally Aspires, and as his Mind is elevated, his Senses grow more refined, and more capable of Delight; his Desires are inlarged, and his Wants increase with his Wishes, which is for everything that is rare, can gratifie his Senses, adorn his Body, and promote the Ease, Pleasure, and Pomp of Life.

Quoted in Appleby, *Economic Thought and Ideology*, 169. Other examples are cited, ibid., 169-75.

14 There is now a large and growing literature on the republican and civic humanist traditions that illuminates the debates on luxury, commerce, and corruption. See especially J.G.A. Pocock, *The Machiavellian Moment: Florentine Political Thought and the Atlantic Republican Tradition* (Princeton: Princeton University Press, 1975), chap. 14; Istvan Hont and Michael Ignatieff, eds., *Wealth and Virtue: The Shaping of Political Economy in the Scottish Enlightenment* (Cambridge: Cambridge University Press, 1983); Albert O. Hirschman, *The Passions and the Interests: Political Arguments for Capitalism before Its Triumph* (Princeton: Princeton University Press, 1977). For a taste of the flavor of civic humanist discourse, see n. 37, below.

15 David Hume, "Of commerce," in *Writings on Economics*, ed. Eugene Rotwein (Madison: University of Wisconsin Press, 1970), 14. For a sensitive treatment of Hume's views on commercial society, see Michael Ignatieff, *The Needs of Strangers: An Essay on Privacy, Solidarity, and the Politics of Being Human* (New York: Viking, Elisabeth Sifton Books, 1985), chap. 3.

16 Hume, "Of commerce," 14-15.

17 Adam Smith, in "Introduction and general plan of the work," *An*

Inquiry into the Nature and Causes of the Wealth of Nations,
ed. R.H. Campbell, A.S. Skinner, and W.B. Todd, 2 vols. (Oxford:
Clarendon Press, 1976), Vol. 1, 10-11, Smith's formulation of the
concept of wealth expresses, in part, the outcome of British
reflection on the sources of Dutch wealth in the seventeenth
century. See Appleby, *Economic Thought and Ideology*, chap. 4.

18   Hume, "Of the populousness of ancient nations," *Writings on
Economics*, 143-7.

19   H. Kalman, "The architecture of mercantilism: commercial
buildings by George Dance the younger," in Paul Fritz and David
Williams, eds., *The Triumph of Culture: 18th Century Perspec-
tives* (Toronto: A.M. Hakkert, 1972), 71.

20   For a general discussion, see Gordon Vichert, "The theory of
conspicuous consumption in the 18th century," in Peter Hughes
and David Williams, eds., *The Varied Pattern: Studies in the
18th Century* (Toronto: A.M. Hakkert, 1971), 253-67; Thomas A.
Horne, *The Social Thought of Bernard Mandeville: Virtue and
Commerce in Early Eighteenth Century England* (New York:
Columbia University Press, 1978), chaps. 1 and 5.

21   David Hume, *A Treatise of Human Nature* (2nd edn), ed. L.A.
Selby-Bigge and P. Neddich (Oxford: Clarendon Press, 1978), 357.

22   Hume, *Treatise*, 365:

> In general we may remark, that the minds of men are mirrors
> to one another, not only because they reflect each others
> emotions, but also because those rays of passions, sentiments
> and opinions may be often reverberated, and may decay away
> by insensible degrees. Thus the pleasure, which a rich man
> receives from his possessions, being thrown upon the be-
> holder, causes a pleasure and esteem; which sentiments again,
> being perceiv'd and sympathiz'd with, encrease the pleasure of
> the possessor; and being once more reflected, become a new
> foundation for pleasure and esteem in the beholder.

23   Hume, *Treatise*, 365.

24   For a discussion of this point, see David Miller, *Philosophy and
Ideology in Hume's Political Thought* (Oxford: Clarendon Press,
1981), chap. 5.

25   Adam Smith, *The Theory of Moral Sentiments*, ed. D.D. Raphael
and A.L. Macfie (Oxford: Clarendon Press, 1976), 182-3.

26   Smith, *Theory of Moral Sentiments*, 182:

The palaces, the gardens, the retinue of the great, are objects of which the obvious conveniency strikes every body. They do not require that their masters should point out to us wherein consists their utility. Of our own accord we readily enter into it, and by sympathy enjoy and thereby applaud the satisfaction which they are fitted to afford him.

27 Smith, *Theory of Moral Sentiments*, 182.
28 Smith, *Theory of Moral Sentiments*, 182.
29 J.H. Plumb, "The commercialization of leisure," in McKendrick, et al., *Birth of a Consumer Society*, 274.
30 Smith, *Theory of Moral Sentiments*, 183.
31 Smith, *Theory of Moral Sentiments*, 50-1.
32 McKendrick, "The consumer revolution," 20-1. See also Roy Porter, *English Society in the Eighteenth Century* (Harmondsworth: Penguin, 1982), chap. 2.
33 Smith, *Lectures on Jurisprudence*, 262.
34 Smith, *Lectures on Jursiprudence*, 208-9.
35 For a discussion of prestige display among the court aristocracy, including the example of counts and dukes, see Norbert Elias, *The Court Society* (New York: Pantheon, 1983), 63-5.
36 Smith, *Theory of Moral Sentiments*, 226. See also Smith, *Wealth of Nations*, 710-14. Thorstein Veblen, *The Theory of the Leisure Class* (Harmondsworth: Penguin, 1979), 86, makes the same point when he observes that:

the means of communication and the mobility of the population now expose the individual to the observation of many persons who have no other means of judging of his reputability than the display of goods (and perhaps of breeding) which he is able to make while he is under their direct observation.

37 Adam Ferguson, seeing this (in 1767), was less sanguine than Smith concerning the prospect of the subtle qualities of birth holding their own against the more easily identifiable and no longer identical qualities of fortune, expressing his fears for republican government in the civic humanist language of virtue and corruption:

nations under a high state of the commercial arts, are exposed to corruption, by their admitting wealth, unsupported by personal elevation and virtue, as the great foundation of distinction, and by having their attention turned on the side of interest, as the road to consideration and honour.

With this effect, luxury may serve to corrupt democratical states, by introducing a species of monarchical subordination, without that sense of high birth and hereditary honours which render the boundaries of rank fixed and determinate, and which teach men to act in their stations with force and propriety. It may prove the occasion of political corruption, even in monarchical governments, by drawing respect towards mere wealth; by casting a shade on the lustre of personal qualities, or family-distinctions; and by infecting all orders of men, with equal venality, servility, and cowardice.

Adam Ferguson, *An Essay on the History of Civil Society* (New Brunswick, N.J. and London: Transaction, 1980), 254-5.

38   McKendrick, "Birth of a Consumer Society," 55-6.

39   Hume, *Treatise*, 365.

40   Hume, *Treatise*, 316-24.

41   Hume acknowledges the importance of comparison in judging relative social standing (*Treatise*, 323), but argues that, as a negative form of evaluation based on distance, it is the opposite of sympathy, a positive evaluation based on the proximity we can gain to the condition of an Other (*Treatise*, 593-5). In Hume's language, then, sympathy outweighs comparison with regard to matters concerning esteem, emulation, and reputation. However, sympathy must extend beyond the socal circle if Hume is to argue that the esteem we feel for riches is universal.

42   Miller, *Philosophy and Ideology in Hume's Political Thought*, 119.

43   Norbert Elias explains that in the seventeenth and eighteenth centuries,

the specifically English stratum of rich bourgeois landowners, the gentry, took a no less eager part in competitive prestige building and status competition than did the leading aristocratic families. And likewise there was a whole number of such families which ruined themselves in this way.

Elias, *Court Society*, 68. See also Fisher, "The development of London as a centre of conspicuous consumption."

44   Veblen, *The Theory of the Leisure Class*, 31.

45   This point concerning Veblen is made also in Arthur O. Lovejoy, *Reflections on Human Nature* (Baltimore: Johns Hopkins Press,

1961), 208-15.

46   Hume, *Treatise*, 484.

47   Hume, *Treatise*, 485.

48   Hume, *Treatise*, 484-501. See also Smith, *Wealth of Nations*, 715 and note. For a discussion that situates the arguments of Smith and Hume regarding justice and property within the tradition of natural jurisprudence as opposed to civic republicanism, see Istvan Hont and Michael Ignatieff, "Needs and justice in the *Wealth of Nations*: an introductory essay," in Hont and Ignatieff, eds., *Wealth and Virtue*.

49   Letter to the Comtesse de Boufflers, dated London, 19 January, 1766, *The Letters of David Hume*, ed. J.Y.T. Greig, 2 vols. (Oxford: Clarendon Press, 1969), 2:1-2.

50   Letter to the Rev. Hugh Blair, dated Lisle Street Leicester Fields, July 1, 1766, *Letters of David Hume*, 2:57.

51   Rousseau's ambivalence, and the creativity that resulted from it, is captured in Robert Darnton, "The social life of Rousseau: anthropology and the loss of innocence," *Harper's*, July 1985, 69-73.

52   Jean-Jacques Rousseau, *The First and Second Discourses and Essay on the Origin of Languages*, ed. and trans. Victor Gourevitch (New York: Harper and Row, 1986), 4-5.

53   Rousseau, *Discourses and Essay*, 5n. For an excellent discussion of Rousseau's theory of needs in comparison with Smith's, see Ignatieff, *The Needs of Strangers*, chap. 4.

54   Rousseau, *Discourses and Essay*, 5-6.

55   Rousseau, *Discourses and Essay*, 150.

56   Rousseau, *Discourses and Essay*, 175.

57   Rousseau, *Discourses and Essay*, 180-1.

58   Rousseau, *Discourses and Essay*, 199.

59   On the ambiguity surrounding Rousseau's conceptualization of society, see Lucio Colletti, "Rousseau as critic of 'civil society'," in *From Rousseau to Lenin: Studies in Ideology and Society* (London: N.L.B., 1972), 164n.

60   Jean-Jacques Rousseau, *Emile, or On Education*, trans. Allan Bloom (New York: Basic Books, 1979), 39:

> We are born with the use of our senses, and from our birth we are affected in various ways by the objects surrounding us. As soon as we have, so to speak, consciousness of our sensations, we are disposed to seek or avoid the objects which produce

them, at first according to whether they are pleasant or unpleasant to us, then according to the conformity or lack of it that we find between us and these objects, and finally according to the judgments we make about them on the basis of the idea of happiness or of perfection given us by reason. These dispositions are extended and strengthened as we become more capable of using our senses and more enlightened; but constrained by our habits, they are more or less corrupted by our opinions. Before this corruption they are what I call in us *nature*.

61   Rousseau, *Emile*, 81.
62   Rousseau, *Emile*, 81.
63   See Ignatieff, *The Needs of Strangers*, 114-18.

2

The promise of abundance

Abundance is the conceptual twin of scarcity. The usages of the two terms run in parallel. When it was still possible to speak of years of scarcity to describe poor yields in the cycle of harvests it was similarly the practice to describe good harvests as years of abundance – there was no implication of linear sequence. Once the experience of scarcity took hold in modernity, abundance took shape as an ideal negation of the present order, appearing in this guise in David Hume's reflections on justice. Eventually, the concept of progress provided a narrative structure within which scarcity and abundance could be accomodated in a single linear frame. Scarcity could then be cast as the antagonist in the human story, a story with a happy ending; the vanquishing of the antagonist and a life of happiness ever after amid abundance for all.

This was not the story told by Hume and Adam Smith. Theirs was a tale, told without pathos, of a perennial struggle with a scarcity that is at once product and producer of our creativity and imagination. Neither comedy nor tragedy, their story was akin to an open-ended myth, giving meaning to the ambiguity of the human condition as they saw it and as their contemporaries experienced it, while dehistoricizing that perception and that experience by universalizing them. But in order to accomplish that universalization, they had recourse to a theory of progress in the form of infinite refinement. Although Hume and Smith refrained from taking it, it was a short step to a conceptualization of history in which progress would provide the mechanism for a deliverance from scarcity, and hence a deliverance from history itself.

The French Revolution, more than any other single episode,

symbolized the possibility of exploding history and served as an impetus to the generation of utopian schemes of all sorts, most of them containing a vision of perfected humanity that then seemed within reach. But the Revolution also set the agenda for the more prosaic politics of the nineteenth century. The terms of political discourse were fundamentally altered and "the social question" was now an unavoidable aspect of European politics. This was no less true of Britain, which had its own revolutionary tradition and where parliamentarism was already established. The extension of political rights to the unpropertied and the question of public responsibility for the poor became central issues of political debate and struggle.

In this setting of historical upheaval, the social order, though basically unchanged, took on a paradoxical aspect it had not seemed to have before. Amid the light of hope and the shadows of fear cast by the Revolution, the simultaneous existence of poverty and affluence began to be perceived as an anomalous situation. The great advances in commerce and industry that were so palpably a legacy of the eighteenth century, and which would become the obsession of the nineteenth, were inextricably bound up with the creation of a universe of desire. Yet the laboring poor were an unmistakable by-product of those advances, and they loomed as unintegrated threats to that universe. In the *Wealth of Nations*, Smith had argued that the unimpeded growth of a commercial society, with its complex division of labor, would carry everyone within it upward through an increase in the general wealth. His point of reference for this claim, however, was situated outside that society. Examining the condition of "the most common artificers or day-labourers in a civilized and thriving country,"[1] Smith observes that,

> Compared, indeed, with the more extravagant luxury of the great, his accommodation must no doubt appear extremely simple and easy; and yet it may be true, perhaps, that the accomodation of an European prince does not always so much exceed that of an industrious and frugal peasant, as the accommodation of the latter exceeds that of many an African king, the absolute master of the lives and liberties of ten thousand naked savages.[2]

But, as we saw in the previous chapter, Smith realized that this external referent is not the basis of comparison upon which a commercial society relies for its emulative dynamic. It is, indeed, the "extravagant luxury," not so much of the great as of the would-be great, that is of immediate relevance to anyone situated in a society with nominally unstable ranks but where the gap between the poor and the lifestyle of desire never seems to close. And so it was that Smith's patient justification gave way to a perceived paradox of poverty amid abundance, a paradox drawn in the relative terms described by historian Eric Hobsbawm, who, acknowledging the dispute over whether or not the laboring poor grew absolutely poorer in the early period of nineteenth-century industrialization, goes on to add:

> There is, of course, no dispute about the fact that *relatively*, the poor grew poorer, simply because the country, and its rich and middle class, so obviously grew wealthier. The very moment when the poor were at the end of their tether – in the early and middle forties – was the moment when the middle class dripped with excess capital, to be wildly invested in railways and spent on the bulging, opulent household furnishings displayed at the Great Exhibition of 1851, and the palatial municipal constructions which prepared to rise in the smoky northern cities.[3]

The Crystal Palace, built to house the 1851 Exhibition, stood as a great display-case for the objects of desire that are at the heart of a society of emulative consumption, but it stood apart from the poor, who, increasingly during the course of the century, occupied their own separated districts of London.[4]

The injustice of poverty amid wealth, intensified by its purposive display, is a recurrent motif of Victorian social critics, from Romantics to Utilitarians, from Chartists to Christian Socialists.[5] Two of those critics, John Stuart Mill and Karl Marx, can be distinguished on the grounds that they devised theories that looked to a process of historical progress that would fundamentally alter the human condition. Both theories entailed a notion of abundance as the necessary precondition for the full realization of human capacities, and each of them established principles of analysis and substantive claims that continue to be evoked today by those who take refuge in the hope of an abundant future to assuage their sense of the injustices of present-day scarcity.

*

It is a measure of the strength exercised by the notion of progress over the minds of nineteenth-century pundits and their readers that the first edition of Thomas Robert Malthus' *Essay on the Principle of Population* (1798), with its dire warning of a perpetual scarcity of food and the consequent impossibility of limitless improvement of the human race, was transformed in its second edition (1803) into a theory of progress. The immediate context for Malthus' first *Essay* had been supplied by two very different sort of events. The first was the bad harvests of 1794-5, a rude reminder of the cyclical patterns of agricultural production that had spurred much reflection on public policy with regard to ensuring food supplies. One such contribution had been Edmund Burke's *Thoughts and Details on Scarcity* (1795), an argument in favor of letting food cycles play themselves out without governmental interference in the form of public assistance.

The second, more far-reaching event to which Malthus was reacting was also, and more famously, a concern of Burke's; namely, the French Revolution, particularly after 1792. One of Malthus' principal intentions in the first *Essay* was to refute ideas concerning the inevitable progress and perfection of the human race, ideas put forward by the Marquis de Condorcet in France and William Godwin (who was also the translator of Condorcet) in England as justifications of the Revolution.[6] While David Hume had postulated a hypothetical condition of abundance in order to establish the grounds of justice in a world of scarcity, Condorcet and Godwin followed out Hume's logic as a practical possibility, arguing that the progress of industry made a future condition of abundance without property or government a realizable utopia. They acknowledged that a time might arrive when the population increase they expected to accompany prosperity could come into conflict with such a vision, but reasoned that such a point was so far off in the future that it need not be of too much concern, particularly since science might well come up with a solution before that point was reached. The nub of Malthus' counterargument is that the necessity for food and sexual desire are two givens of human existence that are perpetually in conflict. In the formulation that is synonymous with his name, "Population, when unchecked, increases in a geometrical ratio. Subsistence increases only in an arithmetical ratio."[7] So from Malthus' perspective, the limit to progress that Condorcet and Godwin consigned to the far-off future is actually an existing and permanent feature of human society, a perpetually reproducing scarcity situation that renders their utopian visions moot. The reality of the human lot is an ever-intensifying competition over food, relieved only by such unintended, "positive" checks on population as famine, high infant mortality rates, war, and other means imposed by nature to reduce surplus mouths, and by the negative check of vice – sex outside the structure of the family or without procreation (including the use of birth control methods).[8]

The first *Essay*'s gloomy view – a gloom that subsequent economic theorizing had difficulty shaking off and that was largely what Thomas Carlyle had in mind when he referred to the "dismal science" – ruled out a state of equilibrium between population and food. Even if nature managed to reduce population temporarily to this level, the lack of want experienced by people would be a great inducement to procreate, starting the geometric curve on its ascendency. But in his revised version, Malthus added something beyond a mass of empirical material meant to buttress his core population theory: he now allowed for "moral restraint" as a check on population along with vice and misery.[9] A virtuous society would be a society without want, one in which population was kept in line with food through the voluntary abstention from sex by enlightened individuals. This now became a vision of social progress, since now society could improve and reach a kind of perfection. Such improvement would be a social, not a natural, process.

John Stuart Mill has given a famous testimony to the influence of Malthus's revised *Essay* on the so-called Philosophic Radicals, the purveyors of Bentham's Utilitarianism:

> Malthus's population principle was quite as much a banner, and point of union among us, as any opinion specially belonging to Bentham. This great doctrine, originally brought forward as an argument against the indefinite improvability of human affairs, we took up with ardent zeal in the contrary sense, as indicating the sole means of realizing that improvability by securing full employment at high wages to the whole labouring population through a voluntary restriction of the increase of their numbers.[10]

The Radicals seized on the prospects of progress through education that Malthus' theory promised, albeit by altering the conception of virtue that lay behind it. Parson Malthus had understood the restraint he called for to be virtuous because it entailed a voluntary abstinence from pleasure. The sublimation of sexual desire in the name of a higher good carried the weight of virtue. The Radicals, on the other hand, jettisoned abstinence in favor of birth control, a less exalted, but presumably more effective means of voluntarily reducing population. Education was the key, but of a different sort than Malthus may have had in mind – J.S. Mill spent a night in jail for distributing birth control pamphlets.[11]

Malthus' somewhat grudging vision of a morally restraining society existing in an equilibrium between population and food, and thus in a condition free from scarcity, provides a fundamental groundwork for John Stuart Mill's later theory of a stationary state. In his influential *Principles of Political Economy* (1848), Mill took issue with those who argued that prosperity and growth were synonymous, claiming that Malthus had exposed the fallacy of this reasoning.[12] Once the ramifications of Malthus's theory are grasped, Mill asserts, the prospect of a levelling off of growth no longer need be feared and should be seen instead for the opportunity it presents to move to a higher level of civilization. For his part, Mill avows that:

> I cannot . . . regard the stationary state of capital and wealth with the unaffected aversion so generally manifested towards it by political economists of the old school. I am inclined to believe that it would be, on the whole, a very considerable improvement on our present condition. I confess I am not charmed with the ideal of life held out by those who think that the normal state of human beings is that of struggling to get on; that the trampling, crushing, elbowing, and treading on each other's heels, which form the existing type of social life, are the most desirable lot of human kind, or anything but the disagreeable symptoms of one of the phases of industrial progress.[13]

When Mill goes on to speculate, somewhat ruefully, that this phase "may be a necessary stage in the progress of civilization,"[14] he has in mind a process in which it is not so much a growth in the productive capacity of a society that is at stake as the development of intellectual faculties that is a by-product of that growth. In an earlier essay entitled, simply, "Civilization" (1836), Mill distinguishes between two meanings of civilization: the first relates to improvement in the highest qualities of human life, to happiness, wisdom, and nobility; the second refers more narrowly to wealth and the improvements related to it.[15] While the attainment of civilization in the first, exalted sense seems to entail the achievement of civilization in the second, crasser form, the reverse is clearly not the case. A society may be wealthy but uncivilized if its inhabitants spend all their time acquiring more wealth and not attending to higher pursuits. In fact, Mill argues strongly that virtually everything in such a society would mitigate against such pursuits, since the only inducement to the exertion of energy

> which can be considered as anything like universal, is the desire of wealth; and wealth being, in the case of the majority, the most accessible means of gratifying all their other desires, nearly the whole of the energy of character which exists in highly civilized societies concentrates itself in the pursuit of that object.[16]

But while a high level of economic development does not make civilization in the broader sense inevitable – indeed, even as it puts up barriers to it – it prepares the ground for it by keeping the mind exercised and by thus expanding the opportunities available to what Mill habitually refers to as "the learned class."

Taking issue with Tocqueville's analysis of the effects of democratic society in his review of the second volume of *Democracy in America* (1840), Mill argues that what Tocqueville describes – the disappearance of the individual into the mass, the instability of social standing, loss of respect for tradition and authority, the dominance of public opinion, etc. – are really the effects of commercial society, not of democracy, since these are all characteristic of England as well as America.[17] Answering Tocqueville's pessimism with his own brand of optimism, Mill finds some hope in the fact that ideas "are themselves a power in history," and therefore "let the idea take hold of the more generous and cultivated minds, that the most serious danger to the future prospects of mankind is in the unbalanced influence of the commercial spirit" and a "national education" could take hold and rescue society.[18] This prospect has a better chance of becoming real in England than in America, Mill thinks, because England has the requisite social structure necessary to produce the needed intellectual atmosphere: "an agricultural class, a leisured class, and a learned class."[19] However, the optimism seems somewhat misplaced, since Mill lays out educational conditions that would have to be met if the agricultural class is to play any role (not to mention his advocacy of this class in part because of its "willingness to look up to, and accept of, guidance"), and since the earlier "Civilization" had despaired of finding such leadership among the enervated leisure class. Only the learned class emerges unscathed and theoretically capable of providing the requisite leadership.

The notion that education can provide the path away from "the existing type of social life" that Mill decries in the *Principles* recalls Rousseau, but with the difference that Mill has transferred the site of education from the individual to the society as a whole, substituting, in effect, the educator for Rousseau's legislator. And there is a Rousseau-like flavor to Mill's description of the inauthenticity of modern life that that education must confront. In "Civilization." Mill observes that the competition endemic to commercial society places appearances at the center of things:

> Success, in so crowded a field, depends not upon what a person is, but upon what he seems: mere marketable qualities become the object instead of substantial ones, and a man's labour and capital are expended less in *doing* anything than in persuading other people that he has done it.[20]

Similarly, in his review of Tocqueville, Mill chides the author for believing that the "entire unfixedness in the social position of individuals – that treading upon the heels of one another – that habitual dissatisfaction of each with the position he occupies, and eager desire to push himself into the next above it" is owing to any peculiarity of America, since the same phenomenon is to be seen in England.[21] This generalized image, too, recalls Rousseau, and helps to reinforce the same sense of the difficulty presented to any scheme for altering the status quo.

But while Mill's educative proposal seems more democratic – or at any rate gentler – than Rousseau's legislative cure, it is so only in appearance and without Rousseau's self-conscious awareness of the contradictions between freedom and necessity entailed in so fundamental an effort at social transformation. The driving force behind Rousseau's *Social Contract* is will; lurking behind Mill's tutelary elite is necessity. When Mill declares in his *Autobiography* that he considered existing institutions to be "merely provisional,"[22] the remark must be understood in the context of the broader notions of progress and scientific theory laid down in the *Principles*. In that work, Mill argues that the principles of economic production are susceptible to scientific formulation, while those of distribution are not. These latter are the product of particular historical and cultural experiences that influence them in precise ways that can be determined in each instance.[23] So while it is possible to scientifically determine why wealth and poverty are distributed in the way that they are in any given society, it is not scientifically valid to say that private property, for example, is economically necessary.[24] An alteration in the habits and customs of a people can lead to an alteration of the distributive pattern in that society. In his mature years, Mill was an active supporter of cooperative enterprises, which he saw as experiments that could help to change attitudes toward work and property. This is consistent with his faith in education and its potential for social transformation. Nevertheless, there is a persistent emphasis on the necessity of economic progress that consistently undercuts Mill's assertions regarding the real possibilities for the success of such educative experiments. Mill detects a progressive evolution of the capacity for cooperation in the gradual increase in production and population that characterizes "civilized" societies, and he pins his hopes and expectations for the future on that capacity.[25] In other words, all the experiments and educative endeavors in the world will fail if there is not a sufficient level of economic development already achieved to buttress them or make them feasible. So while progress is important to Mill's scheme simply because it contributes to a growth of the middle class, the impression is strong that that alone will not suffice; necessity begins to emerge through the cracks in the theory as economic growth begins to assert itself as an absolute precondition to advancement.

Mill's principal capitulation to necessity is in the theory of the stationary state itself. The theory is based on the assumption, made a hypothetical orthodoxy by David Ricardo, of a falling rate of profit.[26] Mill argued that what Ricardo had established as a theoretical possibility could actually occur: as a consequence of a high rate of capital accumulation in a country such as Britain, the rate of profits could fall to virtually zero, ushering in a stationary state.[27] Thus a law of economic growth becomes a necessary prerequisite to the establishment of a social equilibrium in which people could free themselves from the impulse toward competitive accumulation (this being no longer possible for the society as a whole). The social experiments of which Mill was so fond could now play their educative role, since individuals would be searching for some new methods of living their lives. This is Mill's realizable utopia:

> It is scarcely necessary to remark that a stationary condition of capital and population implies no stationary state of human improvement. There would be as much scope as ever for all kinds of mental culture, and moral and social progress; as much room for

improving the Art of Living, and much more likelihood of its being improved, when minds ceased to be engrossed by the art of getting on. Even the industrial arts might be as earnestly and as successfully cultivated, with this sole difference, that instead of serving no purpose but the increase of wealth, industrial improvements would produce their legitimate effect, that of abridging labour. Hitherto it is questionable if all the mechanical inventions yet made have lightened the day's toil of any human being. They have enabled a greater population to live the same life of drudgery and imprisonment, and an increased number of manufacturers and others to make fortunes. They have increased the comforts of the middle classes. But they have not yet begun to effect those great changes in human destiny, which it is in their nature and in their futurity to accomplish. Only when, in addition to just institutions, the increase of mankind shall be under the deliberate guidance of judicious foresight, can the conquests made from the powers of nature by the intellect and energy of scientific discoverers, become the common property of the species, and the means of improving and elevating the universal lot.[28]

This is a post-scarcity utopia – the "Art of Living" refers to quality, not quantity – promising a reduction in labor time and a redistribution of social wealth. It is a vision of abundance wrought by a redefinition of life's needs, but that redefinition would not be possible were it not for the prior exhaustion of a natural process. It is the realization of the natural laws of production, the completion of a process of economic growth that conditions the achievement of a new order of distribution, freeing individuals from the imperatives of a competitive social intercourse necessitated by that growth process. Mill's cooperative utopia is on the far slope of the "necessary stage in the progress of civilization" we are currently in the process of climbing.

Mill bequeathed his theory of a future, rational society of improvement without scarcity to Anglo-American liberalism. It is a theory of social development that follows the pattern of Mill's *Autobiography* and of Victorian autobiography generally. That is a pattern of religious-conversion narrative.[29] In Mill's case, the narrative is a secular one, but the basic structure is consistent with the genre. The autobiographical story is told in three parts: the famous recounting of his early education and acceptance of the Benthamite faith learned from his father, James Mill; the equally famous crisis section dealing with the loss of that faith and the saving effect of his discovery of Wordsworth; and the final period marked by his relationship with Harriet Taylor and his mature works. The Wordsworth episode led directly to his essays on Coleridge and Bentham, essays in which Mill acknowledged the spiritual needs of the human being and decried the Benthamite lack of feeling. But, despite this awakening, Mill's rational impulse always got the better of him, hence his reliance on a combination of enlightened educators and economic progress. His story of social development promises a conversion that follows a similar structure to his own three-part story: the first part is made up of the present competitive scratching and clawing; the second consists of the crisis precipitated by the onset of the stationary state and the collective discovery – with Mill's learned class playing the role of the Romantic poet – that there is more to life; and the final denouement, in which improvement is the guiding light.

The improvement Mill had in mind, as we have seen, was qualitative in nature. His theory accounts for the strength of emulative desire by requiring the realization of a stationary state in order to break its hold. Mill did not, as his Scottish predecessors did, see emulation as related to a human need for recognition, a need which, in modernity, takes the form of external appearances. If he had, he would have had to take emulative competition more seriously in his discussion of the possibilities of cooperation and fair distribution. (Such a consideration accounts, in part, for Tocqueville's relative pessimism.) But emulative competition was recognized by another pupil of Malthus who had a vision of the future inherited from Mill. John Maynard Keynes prophesied, in 1930, that in a century or so, humankind will have surmounted what he called "the economic problem," by which he meant the satisfaction of basic human needs. Throwing off what had been the pursuit of all humanity until then, the human being would then be able to confront "his real, his permanent problem – how to use his freedom from pressing economic cares, how to occupy his leisure, which science and compound interest have won for him, to live wisely and well."[30] This vision of the future is based upon an understanding of need that attempts to take into account the need for recognition:

> Now it is true that the needs of human beings may seem to be insatiable. But they fall into two classes – those needs which are absolute in the sense that we feel them whatever the situation of our fellow human beings may be, and those which are relative in

the sense that we feel them only if their satisfaction lifts us above, makes us feel superior to, our fellows. Needs of the second class, those which satisfy the desire for superiority, may indeed be insatiable; for the higher the general level, the higher still are they. But this is not so true of the absolute needs – a point may soon be reached, much sooner perhaps than we are all of us aware of, when these needs are satisfied in the sense that we prefer to devote our further energies to non-economic purposes.[31]

There is implicit in this formulation the notion that once status competition has ceased to play a functional role in stimulating economic activity it will somehow cease to be of importance, even though it is deemed to be an "insatiable" need. Emulative competition, Keynes suggests, will be transformed automatically once basic material needs are met, because this will entail a transformation in the moral codes by which we have hitherto lived. "We shall be able to rid ourselves of many of the pseudo-moral principles which have hag-ridden us for two hundred years, by which we have exalted some of the most distasteful of human qualities into the position of the highest virtues," Keynes wrote, reminiscent of Mill. But then he went on in language more extreme than Mill could muster, and more characteristic of his Bloomsbury milieu, to foretell that "the love of money as a possession . . . will be recognized for what it is, a somewhat disgusting morbidity, one of those semi-criminal, semi-pathological propensities which one hands over with a shudder to the specialists in mental disease."[32] The new dispensation will mean that while there still may be some who are foolish or misguided enough to pursue the accumulation of wealth, "the rest of us will no longer be under any obligation to applaud and encourage them."[33] Instead, freed from the functional necessity imposed by the dynamics of material need satisfaction, emulation can shift its ground and "we shall honour those who can teach us how to pluck the hour and the day virtuously and well."[34]

Keynes' invocation of an "obligation" currently governing social emulation is a telling one. While David Hume and Adam Smith attributed a functional role in the workings of an economy to social emulation, they did not argue that that emulation takes place *because* of its functional use. Nor did they argue that it could be set aside once some level of need satisfaction was reached. Their conception of need was such that need is always seen as socially defined, and part of that definition in a commercial society is

constituted by emulative desire. Indeed, Hume and Smith, as well as
Rousseau, effectively argue that in modernity need becomes desire,
and so it is an error to suppose that satiety can be reached because
desire does not come to rest on any particular object. The essence of
desire is movement; it is, strictly speaking, objectless. Keynes can
envision a transcendence of the present only because he separates
need from desire and assumes that desire is functionally related to the
satisfaction of need. Need then becomes more or less a fixed quantity
while desire can be wished away.

The tradition that begins with Malthus and incorporates Mill and
Keynes is one that combines a critical stance *vis-à-vis* the social
patterns and motivations of modern economies with a promise that it
can be different in the future. That critical stance is sometimes a
moral one (Malthus), sometimes an aesthetic one (Keynes), and
sometimes both (Mill). The promise is in each case based on the
presumption that the distasteful present is a necessary precursor to
the attractive future. And in each case, the present and past are
explained in terms of a necessary struggle with scarcity that will yield
a future of abundance. In a curious way, then, this tradition, which
sets out to criticize the status quo, winds up offering a legitimation
for it. Although not arguing that the present way of life is the only
possible way of life, Mill and Keynes do end up arguing that it is the
only possible one under present material circumstances.

*

The promise of abundance is also the product of the nineteenth
century's most powerful antimalthusian theory and the tradition that
flows from it. In rejecting Malthus' population theory on the grounds
that its author had obscured the historically specific relations that
lead to overpopulation in any particular case by generating a spurious
natural law of population,[35] Karl Marx displays several salient
characteristics of the style and substance of his thought. Chief among
these is a critical historicism, which, when combined with Marx's
philosophy of history, allows him to consistently criticize political
economy for mistakenly universalizing the economic laws of a
capitalist system while resituating those laws within a broader
sequence of necessary historical stages. Thus, while Marx denies the
necessity of the phenomena political economy describes in its terms,
he restores that necessity in his own terms. In the case of population,

Marx replaces Malthus' explanation with his own: it is the limitations that have always and everywhere been placed on production that account for overpopulation. Remove those constraints and the problem of overpopulation will be consigned (along with capitalism, the latest system of restraint) to history's garbage heap. Population, as such, is no barrier to the achievement of abundance.

Marx's steadfast awareness of the historical character of social relations, and of the tendency demonstrated by contemporary theorists to naturalize those relations, is what sets him off from the apostles of progress who were Malthus' initial targets. And yet, Marx's own progressivist philosophy of history gets the better of his historicism, ensuring that his version of the human story will come out bearing the same structure as Mill's *Autobiography*. In Marx's telling, the three component stages are history (or what Marx sometimes refers to as "prehistory"), revolution, and the society of true humanity (the "society of associated producers"). Scarcity is a phenomenon of the first stage; the last stage presupposes its transcendence. This presupposition, however, is not a simple one. It is based on a complicated, ultimately self-defeating conceptualization of human needs.[36]

Like those of the Scottish theorists of the eighteenth century, Marx's understanding of needs is one in which all needs are seen as social. In *The German Ideology* (1845-6), Marx and his coauthor Frederick Engels argue that "life involves before everything else eating and drinking, a habitation, clothing and many other things. The first historical act is thus the production of the means to satisfy these needs, the production of material life itself."[37] However, these fundamental needs can be satisfied in a variety of particular ways. The particular means utilized themselves become new needs, since they have to be produced in order to satisfy the original needs, and so Marx and Engels, in what amounts to a clarification of the first statement, immediately add that "this production of new needs is the first historical act."[38] In this formulation, history is the history of need.

As in Rousseau's anthropology of need, this conception is one in which the history of need is one of domination (of nature by human beings and of human beings by themselves). But unlike Rousseau's critique of social needs, Marx's version looks to the inherently expansionary character of need thus understood for a notion of the expanding capacities of the human being, capacities which, when unleashed in a nonoppressive context and after a long period of development, will signal the realization of true humanity. Marx's *Economic and Philosophical Manuscripts* (1844), which went unpublished until 1932, contain a vehement attack on what Marx calls "crude communism," the doctrine of those whom he sees as reacting to the paradox of poverty amid wealth with a simplistic call for a leveling down of social classes. Such an approach is criticized by Marx as being nothing more than a reflex negation of the present order, where envy rules desire and where everyone, no matter how rich, seeks to pull down those who are richer still. The crude communist simply substitutes an absolute minimum level to which all will be reduced, by abolishing private property, for the relative leveling characteristic of the competition of the system of private property. Marx comments:

> How little this abolition of private property is a true appropriation is shown by the abstract negation of the entire world of culture and civilization, and the return to the *unnatural* simplicity of the *poor*, unrefined man who has no needs and who has not even reached the stage of private property let alone gone beyond it.[39]

In contrast, Marx understands contemporary society to be in the grips of a necessary but perverse "system of needs," as his great predecessor Hegel termed civil society, that develops human needs unequally and irrationally. The solution lies not in leveling down, but in going beyond this system to one where needs can develop freely as the birthright of all.

Marx's criticism of what would later be called capitalism is driven by a notion of historical progress that leads him to reject crude communism as regressive. The human being is understood by him to be an historical project, one in which the creativity of the species leads to greater refinement in taste, to the creation of new needs that result from that refinement, and to the fuller development of the human senses, whose own refinement is tied to the progressively more refined objects created by and for new needs.[40] The creation of objects is thus a need unto itself, since it is through such creative power that human beings realize themselves as sensuous beings. "The whole of history," Marx therefore claims, "is a preparation, a development, for 'man' to become the object of *sensuous* consciousness and for the needs of 'man as man' to become [sensuous] needs."[41]

The system of private property described by political economy is one stage in that history, a stage in which some people are given the means with which to develop their needs to a highly refined degree while vast numbers of others are reduced to inhuman conditions.[42] Indeed, Marx points out, in the framework of political economy, where not felt need but effective demand – the actual ability to remove goods from the market – is all that matters, the poor have no needs because they do not have the capacity to turn need into demand: they have no money, the only language of need markets understand.[43] The private property system, while aiding in the growth of sensual life through the creation of objects to satisfy effective demand, simultaneously distorts that growth by ignoring the silent human needs of the poor and by the manipulation of needs on the market. Marx's attack on this latter point is an echo of Rousseau:

> Each person speculates on creating a *new* need in the other, with the aim of forcing him to make a new sacrifice, placing him in a new dependence and seducing him into a new kind of *enjoyment* and hence into economic ruin. Each attempts to establish over the other an alien power, in the hope of thereby achieving satisfaction of his own selfish needs. With the mass of objects grows the realm of alien powers to which man is subjected, and each new product is a new *potentiality* of mutual fraud and mutual pillage.[44]

Marx repeatedly has recourse to the relationship between prostitute, pimp, and john to characterize such a system.

That characterization points to the belief that these manipulated needs are inauthentic or exploitative; they are somehow not "true" or "real" needs. But authentic needs remain unspecified, an ideal for the future that serves only as a somewhat nebulous critical measure in the present. What makes the needs that appear in capitalism inauthentic is that they are intentionally created in people for the purpose of realizing profit; they are the needs of capital, not of autonomous human beings.[45] But these false needs serve a higher purpose by providing capital with the markets necessary for its expansion, and thus by helping to create the productive capacity necessary for the transcendence of capitalism and the creation of a "society of associated producers" that would be the articulation of real human needs.

As Marx's comments on crude communism in the *Economic and*

Philosophical Manuscripts illustrate, the developmental logic that underlies his conception of need entails a notion of necessary stages that must be traversed before the promise of human fulfillment can be realized. In the absence of a sufficiently high degree of economic development, Marx insists in the *German Ideology*, such a realization is impossible, "because without it *want* is merely made general, and with *destitution* the struggle for necessities and all the old filthy business would necessarily be reproduced."[46] That capitalism paves the way to a future without want is announced with great rhetorical flair in the *Communist Manifesto* (1848), which can be read as a funeral oration delivered by an old enemy who has arrived not to bury but to praise. The bourgeoisie, the subjective embodiment of capitalism, has wrought a revolution:

> It has been the first to show what man's activity can bring about. It has accomplished wonders far surpassing Egyptian pyramids, Roman aqueducts, and Gothic cathedrals; it has conducted expeditions that put in the shade all former Exoduses of nations and crusades.[47]

And it has brought about these great accomplishments on a world-wide scale as its search for markets has led to the penetration of every border and the subsequent forced transformation of all economies into capitalist ones, with all that that implies.[48] In a passage rivalling any ever written by Andrew Carnegie for its sheer delight in capitalism's power, Marx and Engels unleash their praise:

> The bourgeoisie, during its rule of scarce one hundred years, has created more massive and more colossal productive forces than have all preceding generations together. Subjection of Nature's forces to man, machinery, application of chemistry to industry and agriculture, steam-navigation, railways, electric telegraphs, clearing of whole continents for cultivation, canalisation of rivers, whole populations conjured out of the ground – what earlier century had even a presentiment that such productive forces slumbered in the lap of social labour?[49]

It is in this great productive power, and in its universal spread, that Marx sees a future without "all the old filthy business."

That future of abundance entails an escape from necessity into freedom, but not the complete suppression of necessity. Marx foresees a working day reduced to its barest minimum, allowing for the material reproduction of society, but also allowing for the expansion of free time, during which the authentic needs of people can be discovered and acted upon.[50] This notion suggests that lurking behind Marx's view of need is a conception of material needs as at least potentially fixed, but such a conception is difficult to maintain within the terms of his own understanding of need. In discussing capitalism's thirst for profits in *Capital*, Marx remarks that economic systems oriented toward the satisfaction of use values are inherently limited in their scope, whereas market systems oriented toward the accumulation of monetary wealth are not, an insight he correctly attributes to Aristotle.[51] However, unlike Aristotle, who worked with a conception of needs as natural, Marx understands needs as being social in composition. When he argues that capitalists seek to push wages down to a subsistence level, he adds that subsistence is socially determined – what is regarded as minimal subsistence by one generation may not be so regarded by another.[52] This social determination of material need would not cease with the end of capitalism, since Marx posits a continued development of productive forces, creating a continued rise in the socially defined level of minimal material need. "Just as the savage must wrestle with Nature to satisfy his wants, to maintain and reproduce life, so must civilized man, and he must do so in all social formations and under all possible modes of production," Marx writes in the third volume of *Capital*, invoking an historical law communism cannot abrogate. "With his development his realm of physical necessity expands as a result of his wants; but, at the same time, the forces of production which satisfy these wants also increase." The increase of material wants will continue under communism, but the process of generating and satisfying them will be brought under collective, rationalized control.[53]

So it seems that even though Marx envisions a continuing spiral of new material needs under communism, he does not see this spiral affecting the amount of time necessary to satisfy these needs; even though new material needs will be continually generated, necessary labor time can be reduced to a minimum, allowing the free time necessary for cultivating the needs of the spirit. But if material needs are social, rather than natural, they are also relative. Marx acknowledges this in *Wage Labour and Capital* (1849), where he points out that a person who lives in a small house is satisfied "as long as the surrounding houses are equally small," and that small house then suffices to satisfy the material need for shelter. But, let a palace arise beside the little house, and it shrinks from a little house to a hut. The little house shows now that its owner has only very slight or no demands to make; and however high it may shoot up in the course of civilization, if the neighbouring palace grows to an equal or even greater extent, the occupant of the relatively small house will feel more and more uncomfortable, dissatisfied and cramped within its four walls.

Drawing an analogy with the increase in wages that historically accompanied the development of capitalism, Marx goes on to remark that,

the rapid growth of productive capital brings about an equally rapid growth of wealth, luxury, social wants, social enjoyments. Thus although the enjoyments of the workers have risen, the social satisfaction that they give has fallen in comparison with the increased enjoyments of the capitalist, which are inaccessible to the worker, in comparison with the state of development of society in general.

This example, Marx continues, shows that "our desires and pleasures spring from society; we measure them, therefore, by society and not by the objects which serve for their satisfaction. Because they are of a social nature, they are of a relative nature."[54]

But if there is no natural limit to desire, and if desire is necessarily bound up with what Veblen called invidious comparison, then a society predicated on the transcendence of want would appear to be impossible.[55] This is true even if we follow G.A. Cohen's caution that "the promise of abundance is not an endless flow of goods but a sufficiency produced with a minimum of unpleasant exertion,"[56] since the notion of a sufficiency is itself posited by Marx as socially – that is to say, comparatively – determined. Marx can foresee a communist society of abundance only because he retains the substantively empty notion of "authentic" needs in the domain of material wants that acts as a limitation his general theory of need denies.[57]

The Marxist tradition has carried the master's theory of the transcendence of scarcity forward in two opposing directions. One line, best exemplified in philosophy by Herbert Marcuse, has reveled in the liberatory possibilities of capitalism's productive technology, even while decrying its contemporary effects, and can be called the utopian road. Relying on a version of Marx's authentic needs, the utopians see a potential surplus under current conditions if only the creation of false needs were to end and labor-saving technology be fully exploited [58]. The other direction, put into practice in the Soviet Union and its dominions, has sought to suppress desire in order to hasten the arrival of communist abundance. This increasingly discredited path represents the dystopian route, a twentieth-century version of a Rousseau-like revolution from above against scarcity.

Marx's attempt to base a critical theory of capitalism – one which entails its supercession – on the ground of a theory of need collapses once the claim that all needs are social in composition is taken seriously. As we have seen in the discussion of the Scottish theorists, of Rousseau, and of Mill and Keynes, such an interpretation of need reveals that needs cannot be separated from desire in the modern mentality. Among the (necessarily) unfulfilled desires that modernity creates is the desire for abundance, and Marx's theory, like Mill's, is one manifestation of that desire.

*

While the apostles of progress either reveled in or tolerated the smokestacks of production and the showcases of consumption, there were among the Victorian moral critics those who were unwilling to countenance these markers of the promise of abundance. The voices of Thomas Carlyle, John Ruskin, and William Morris united over the course of the nineteenth century in a dissonant chorus of Romantic protest against that unfulfilled promise. Unlike their progressivist contemporaries, J.S. Mill and Karl Marx, the Romantic radicals rejected the notion of historical necessity that justified scarcity in the present in the hope of abundance in the future, but they did not reject the notion of abundance itself. Instead, they sought to alter the metaphors through which society and history were understood, and in so doing to alter the actions of men and women, resulting in a fundamentally transformed society in which abundance would be realized immediately.

Carlyle, in *Past and Present* (1843), described "the condition of England" in terms that signaled the Romantic attitude toward a squandered abundance:

England is full of wealth, of multifarious produce, supply for human want in every kind; yet England is dying of inanition. With unabated bounty the land of England blooms and grows; waving with yellow harvests; thick-studded with workshops, industrial implements, with fifteen millions of workers, understood to be the strongest, the cunningest and the willingest our Earth ever had; these men are here; the work they have done, the fruit they have realised is here, abundant, exuberant on every hand of us: and behold, some baleful fiat as of Enchantment has gone forth, saying, "Touch it not, ye workers, ye master-workers, ye master-idlers; none of you can touch it, no man of you shall be the better for it; this is enchanted fruit!"[59]

The paradox of poverty and plenty that has beguiled the modern age is seen here not as the result of a historical grand plan whose logic we should attempt to grasp but as a consequence of a combination of unjust distribution and a warped sense of life's purpose. "In Poor and Rich," Carlyle observes, "instead of noble thrift and plenty, there is idle luxury alternating with mean scarcity and inability. We have sumptuous garnitures for our Life, but have forgotten to *live* in the middle of them. It is an enchanted wealth."[60] Governed by a "Gospel of Mammonism" that dictates the pursuit of monetary wealth at the expense of all social ties other than the "Cash-payment," the inhabitants of market societies are in the grip of an enchantment that prevents their seeing the possibility of living otherwise.[61]

The Romantic model of another way of living is essentially medieval and aesthetic in inspiration. The Romantics employed a premodern metaphor of organicism against the prosaic atomism and mechanistic metaphors of modernity, which they identified with British political economy.[62] Carlyle structured *Past and Present* in this way, counterposing observations on his contemporary scene with meditations on the twelfth-century life of the Abbey of St. Edmunsbury, as gleaned from the "Boswellian Notebook" of one of its monks, Jocelin of Brakelond, and from Carlyle's own visit to the abbey's ruins. Ruskin's chapter on "The Nature of Gothic" in *The Stones of Venice* (1851-3), itself of enormous influence on Morris, carried forward this approach, as did Morris' romances and his utopian *News from Nowhere*, which described a future society in medieval terms.

The penchant for medieval examples and models expresses the Romantic insistence on taking things whole; on understanding everything in terms of an ordered unity constituted by parts that are often in conflict but which add up to a harmonious totality. Ruskin's appreciation of the imperfection in the execution of detail and ornament in Gothic building is an instance of such a view.[63] This organic conceptualization bears some superficial resemblance to Adam Smith's notion of a social order constituted through unintentional actions and motivations, but the Romantics were at pains to argue that the conflict and tension they perceived in the composition of the whole was not the same thing as competition in the marketplace. Disdainful of the effects of competition on human solidarity, the Romantics were unwilling to accept as legitimate the value of the second-order happiness in possessions and the esteem associated with them that Smith had seen as the best one could hope for in society.

In having recourse to a premodern, organicist conception of society and its composition, the Romantics applied a premodern notion of political economy to their reflections on abundance. Rather than adopting classical political economy's Smithian idea of wealth as the proliferation of goods, the Romantics thought in terms of wise management of one's labor and consumption, within an overall order of nature and society. Ruskin was the most explicit of the Romantics on this point, arguing in his "Political economy of art" (1857) that:

> the world is so regulated by the laws of Providence, that a man's labour, well applied, is always amply sufficient to provide him during his life with all things needful to him, and not only with those, but with many pleasant objects of luxury; and yet farther, to procure him large intervals of healthful rest and serviceable leisure. And a nation's labour, well applied, is in like manner, amply sufficient to provide its whole population with good food and comfortable habitation; and not with those only, but with good education besides, and objects of luxury, art treasures. . . . But by those same laws of Nature and Providence, if the labour of the nation or of the individual be misapplied, and much more if it be insufficient, – if the nation or man be indolent and unwise, – suffering and want result.[64]

This formulation is recognized by Ruskin to be Greek in inspiration – a literal translation of *economia* as household management – and harkens back to Scholastic thinking on material life. As such, it was particularly serviceable as a theoretical vantage point for an attack on the emulative, acquisitive framework of commercial society, which could be interpreted as out of control, heedless of the limitations imposed by a natural order. In such an order, individuals find their identity in the expressive character of their work and in the position they occupy within the whole, rather than, as in commercial society, in the sham externalities of riches. From the Romantic perspective, the present system, dominated by what Ruskin referred to as the "Goddess of Getting-on," appears as a historical oddity with profoundly dehumanizing implications. Here scarcity is seen as a *sui generis* invention of the modern age.

Among the Romantics, Ruskin is the most consistent in denying any hint of necessity to historical development. Both Carlyle and Morris occasionally nod in the direction of claims that industry and economic progress have now made possible the abundance which is being squandered, a position that would bring them closer to Marx and make their arguments susceptible to the same threat of delayed gratification. But Ruskin's more fully articulated theory of political economy allows him to follow through on the implications of the Romantic critique and to argue that another way of life is available at any moment, provided only that the will is sufficiently strong and the eyes sufficiently capable of seeing. For Ruskin, the medieval example shows that history is not continuous, that it has no overriding logic to which we must subject ourselves, that a radical rupture is possible.[65]

The radical quality of that rupture is signaled by the medieval imagery the Romantics deploy. That imagery plays a disruptive role in their writing, urging their readers to see the present anew. In this regard, they can be distinguished from some other critics – Edmund Burke and William Cobbet come to mind – who, earlier in the century, also criticized the new industrial and commercial society, but did so from the point of view of the recent past, or at least of the imagination of it. Though the Romantics may have been appealing to the same sense of loss in personal or collective experience as Burke or Cobbet, they took seriously Carlyle's notion that society was in a state of enchantment, which precluded a direct appeal. People had to be jolted out of a way of seeing themselves, others, and nature that had become all too natural to them. By going further into the past for their images and inspiration, and by driving them home linguistically through the use of powerful metaphors, the Romantics hoped to provide that jolt. In addition, Ruskin and Morris attempted to give expression to their ideas about work and economy – to teach by example Ruskin's dictum in *Unto this Last* (1862) that "There is no Wealth but Life" – in Ruskin's plans for the St. George's Guild[66] and in Morris' craft workshops.

The practical difficulties entailed in the Romantic attitude toward scarcity are based in this need to radically deny fundamental aspects of daily, lived experience. That experience was one of insufficiency. The Romantics, unlike the theorists of progress, could not promise a different future that would make the present scrambling worthwhile – they held out the prospect of an altered present that hinged on the subsumption of desire within an ordered whole. Their championing of an aesthetic existence as the antidote to the endless pursuit of material wealth, their insistence on the need for a form of reason that deduced the means of life from the ends of life, has labeled them "sages," "seers," "prophets." Often used perjoratively, to signify the unreality of their vision when compared with the quotidian reality of modernity, these terms express the radicalness of their temperament and their uncompromising rejection of the enchanting Goddess of Getting-on.

NOTES

1 Adam Smith, *An Inquiry into the Nature and Causes of the Wealth of Nations*, ed. R.H. Campbell, A.S. Skinner, and W.B. Todd, 2 vols. (Oxford: Clarendon Press, 1976), Vol. 1, 22.

2 Smith, *Wealth of Nations*, 23-4. Smith's discussion of inequality as a necessity for the betterment of the conditions of the poor is itself treated as the articulation of a paradox in Istvan Hont and Michael Ignatieff, "Needs and justice in the *Wealth of Nations*: an introductory essay," in Hont and Ignatieff, eds., *Wealth and Virtue: The Shaping of Political Economy in the Scottish Englightenment* (Cambridge: Cambridge University Press, 1983), 1-44.

3 E.J. Hobsbawm, *Industry and Empire* (New York: Pantheon, 1968), 72.

4 Gareth Stedman Jones, *Outcast London: A Study in the Relationship between Classes in Victorian Society* (Harmondsworth: Penguin, Peregrine Books, 1976), 13.

5 Some representative texts have been conveniently collected in Elisabeth Jay and Richard Jay, eds., *Critics of Capitalism: Victorian Reactions to 'Political Economy'* (Cambridge: Cambridge University Press, 1986).

6 For the background to Malthus' first *Essay*, see Elie Halevy, *The Growth of Philosophic Radicalism* (Clifton, N.J.: Augustus M. Kelley, 1972), 225-48. For a discussion of Malthus' population theory within the broader context of his political and economic writings, see Stefan Collini, Donald Winch, and John Burrow, *That Noble Science of Politics: A Study in Nineteenth-Century Intellectual History* (Cambridge: Cambridge University Press, 1983), chap. 2.

7 Thomas Robert Malthus, *On Population*, ed. Gertrude Himmelfarb (New York: Modern Library, 1960), 9.

8 In discussing the imperatives men take into consideration in contemplating having a family, Malthus includes a Humean calculation of social status:

> A man of liberal education, but with an income only just sufficient to enable him to associate in the rank of gentlemen, must feel absolutely certain that if he marries and has a family he shall be obliged, if he mixes at all in society, to rank himself with moderate farmers and the lower classes of tradesmen. The woman that a man of education would naturally make the object of his choice would be one brought up in the same tastes and sentiments with himself and used to the familiar intercourse of a society totally different from that to which she must be reduced by marriage. Can a man consent to place the object of his affection in a situation so discordant, probably, to her tastes and inclinations? Two or three steps of descent in society, particularly at this round of the ladder, where education ends and ignorance begins, will not be considered by the generality of people as a fancied and chimerical, but a real and essential evil. If society be held desireable, it surely must be free, equal, and reciprocal society, where benefits are conferred as well as received, and not such as the dependent finds with his patron or the poor with the rich.

Malthus, *On Population*, 26-7.

9 Malthus, *On Population*, 477-86.

10 John Stuart Mill, *Autobiography* (Indianapolis: Library of Liberal Arts, 1957), 68. See also Mill's comments in his unfinished "Chapters on Socialism" (1879) where he claims that progress has diminished the threat of overpopulation:

> experience shows that in the existing state of society the

pressure of population on subsistence, which is the principal cause of low wages, though a great, is not an increasing evil; on the contrary, the progress of all that is called civilisation has a tendency to diminish it, partly by the more rapid increase of the means of employing and maintaining labour, partly by the increased facilities opened to labour for transporting itself to new countries and unoccupied fields of employment, and partly by a general improvement in the intelligence and prudence of the population.

John Stuart Mill, *Essays on Economics and Society*, ed. J.M. Robson (Toronto and Buffalo: University of Toronto Press, 1967), 729.

11   Bernard Semmel, *John Stuart Mill and the Pursuit of Virtue* (New Haven: Yale University Press, 1984), 27-9.

12   Mill's appeal to Malthus appears at the outset of his discussion "Of the stationary state":

The doctrine that, to however distant a time incessant struggling may put off our doom, the progress of society must "end in shallows and in miseries," far from being, as many people still believe, a wicked invention of Mr. Malthus, was either expressly or tacitly affirmed by his most distinguished predecessors, and can only be successfully combated on his principles. Before attention had been directed to the principle of population as the active force in determining the remuneration of labor, the increase of mankind was virtually treated as a constant quantity; it was, at all events, assumed that in the natural and normal state of human affairs population must constantly increase, from which it followed that a constant increase of the means of support was essential to the physical comfort of the mass of mankind. The publication of Mr. Malthus' Essay is the era from which better views of this subject must be dated; and notwithstanding the acknowledged errors of his first edition, few writers have done more than himself, in the subsequent editions, to promote these juster and more hopeful anticipations.

John Stuart Mill, *Principles of Political Economy*, ed. J.M. Robson (Toronto and Buffalo: University of Toronto Press, 1965), 753.

13   Mill, *Principles*, 753-4.

14   Mill, *Principles*, 754.

15   John Stuart Mill, *Essays on Politics and Culture*, ed. Gertrude

Himmelfarb (1962; reprint, Glouster, Mass.: Peter Smith, 1973),
45.

16 Mill, *Essays on Politics and Culture*, 56.

17 John Stuart Mill, "Tocqueville on Democracy in America (vol.
II)," *Essays on Politics and Culture*, 257-67.

18 Mill, *Essays on Politics and Culture*, 264.

19 Mill, *Essays on Politics and Culture*, 264.

20 Mill, *Essays on Politics and Culture*, 60.

21 Mill goes on to argue that if the American example shows
anything that could not be learned from the English experience it
is that "the 'sabbathless pursuit of wealth' could be as intensely
prevalent, where there were no aristocratic distinctions to tempt
it." Mill, *Essays on Politics and Culture*, 259.

22 Mill, *Autobiography*, 150.

23 Mill, *Principles*, 20-1. For a criticism based on Mill's inability to
sustain this distinction within the *Principles*, see James Bonar,
Philosophy and Political Economy, 3rd edn (New York: Humanities Press; London: George Allen & Unwin, 1967), 252-8.

24 In his "Chapters on Socialism," Mill makes the further point
that "the idea of property is not some one thing, identical
throughout history and incapable of alteration, but is variable
like all other creations of the human mind." Mill, Essays on
Economics and Society, 753.

25 Mill, *Principles*, 707-9.

26 Joseph A. Schumpeter, *History of Economic Analysis* (New York:
Oxford University Press, 1954), 682-5.

27 Mill, *Principles*, 738-41.

28 Mill, *Principles*, 756-7.

29 See Jerome Hamilton Buckley, *The Turning Key: Autobiography
and the Subjective Impulse since 1800* (Cambridge, Mass.:
Harvard University Press, 1984), 77-81.

30 John Maynard Keynes, "Economic possibilities for our grand-
children," in *Essays in Persuasion* (New York and London: W. W.
Norton, 1963), 367.

31 Keynes, *Essays in Persuasion*, 365.

32 Keynes, *Essays in Persuasion*, 369.

33 Keynes, *Essays in Persuasion*, 370.

34 Keynes, *Essays in Persuasion*, 372. Keynes' forecast is taken up
and made a possibility for the present by C.B. Macpherson, *The
Real World of Democracy* (New York: Oxford University Press,

1966), 61-5, where he argues that scarcity is an outdated legitimating principle of market societies, no longer functionally necessary for the production and distribution of material goods.

35   Karl Marx, *Grundrisse: Foundations of the Critique of Political Economy (Rough Draft)*, trans. Martin Nicolaus (London: Allen Lane, 1973), 605-6:

> [Malthus'] conception is altogether false and childish ... because he regards *overpopulation* as being *of the same kind* in all the different historical phases of economic development; does not understand their specific difference, and hence stupidly reduces these very complicated and varying relations to a single relation, two equations, in which the natural reproduction of humanity appears on the one side, and the natural reproduction of edible plants (or means of subsistence) on the other, as two natural series, the former geometric and the latter arithmetic in progression. In this way he transforms the historically distinct relations into an abstract numerical relation, which he has fished purely out of thin air, and which rests neither on natural nor on historical laws.

36   The best case for a coherent conceptualization is made by Agnes Heller, *The Theory of Need in Marx* (London: Allison & Busby, 1976). Her interpretation is challenged by Patricia Springborg, *The Problem of Human Needs and the Critique of Civilization* (London: George Allen & Unwin, 1981), 198-213. See also Jon Elster, *Making Sense of Marx* (Cambridge: Cambridge University Press, 1985), 68-92.

37   Karl Marx and Frederick Engels, *The German Ideology* (Moscow: Progress Publishers, 1968), 39.

38   Marx and Engels, *German Ideology*, 40. Marshall Sahlins, *Culture and Practical Reason* (Chicago: University of Chicago Press, 1978), 47-50, points out that in other texts Marx advances the idea that primitive societies are a part of nature, not history, a distinction that is based upon the view that primitive societies reproduce rather than augment their limited needs.

39   Karl Marx, *Early Writings*, trans. Rodney Livingstone and Gregor Benton (Harmondsworth: Penguin, 1975), 346.

40   Marx, *Early Writings*, 353.

41   Marx, *Early Writings*, 355.

42   "It is true that labour produces marvels for the rich, but it produces privation for the worker. It produces palaces, but hovels

for the worker. It produces beauty, but deformity for the worker. . . . It produces intelligence, but it produces idiocy and cretinism for the worker." Marx, *Early Writings*, 325-6. See G.A. Cohen, *Karl Marx's Theory of History: A Defence* (Princeton: Princeton University Press, 1978), 204-6.

43 Marx, *Early Writings*, 378.

44 Marx, *Early Writings*, 358.

45 See Heller, *The Theory of Need in Marx*, 51-2.

46 Marx and Engels, *German Ideology*, 47.

47 Karl Marx and Frederick Engels, "Manifesto of the Communist Party," in Karl Marx and Frederick Engels, *Selected Works* (New York: International Publishers, 1968), 38.

48 That Marx and Engels do not see this development in a wholly negative light is evident in the following:

> The bourgeoisie, by the rapid improvement of all instruments of production, by the immensely facilitated means of communication, draws all, even the most barbarian, nations into civilisation. The cheap prices of its commodities are the heavy artillery with which it batters down all Chinese walls, with which it forces the barbarians' intensely obstinate hatred of foreigners to capitulate. It compels all nations, on pain of extinction, to adopt the bourgeois mode of production; it compels them to introduce what it calls civilisation into their midst, i.e., to become bourgeois themselves. In one word, it creates a world after its own image.
>
> The bourgoisie has subjected the country to the rule of the towns. It has created enormous cities, has greatly increased the urban population as compared with the rural, and has thus rescued a considerable part of the population from the idiocy of rural life. Just as it has made the country dependent on the towns, so it has made barbarian and semi-barbarian countries dependent on the civilised ones, nations and peasants on nations of bourgeois, the East on the West.

Marx and Engels, "Manifesto," 39. Among other things, bringing the "rural idiots" and "barbarians" into urban civilization would mean bringing them into the world of desire.

49 Marx and Engels, "Manifesto," 39-40.

50 G.A. Cohen emphasizes this aspect of Marx's theory, neatly summarizing its logic:

> The productive technology of advanced capitalism begets an

unparalleled opportunity of lifting the curse of Adam and liberating men from toil, but the production relations of capitalist economic organization prevents the opportunity from being seized. The economic form most able to relieve toil is least disposed to do so. In earlier periods of capitalist history the bias toward output conferred on the system a progressive historical role: capitalism was an indispensable engine for producing material wealth from a starting point of scarcity, and there lay its 'historical justification'. But as scarcity recedes the same bias renders the system reactionary. It cannot realize the possibilities of liberation it creates. It excludes liberation by febrile product innovation, huge investments in sales and advertising, contrived obsolescence. It brings society to the threshold of abundance and locks the door. For the promise of abundance is not an endless flow of goods but a sufficiency produced with a minimum of unpleasant exertion.

Cohen, *Marx's Theory of History*, 306-7.

51 Karl Marx, *Capital*, vol. 1, trans. Samuel Moore and Edward Aveling (Moscow: Progress Publishers, n.d.), 150-1 and 150n.

52 Marx, *Capital*, vol. 1, 168.

53 Karl Marx, *Capital*, vol. 3 (Moscow: Progress Publishers, 1971), 820.

54 Karl Marx, "Wage labour and capital," Marx and Engels, *Selected Works*, 84-5.

55 Commenting on this passage from *Wage Labour and Capital*, Springborg notes:

Marx's admission that there is a psychological aspect to needs casts a shadow over the hope that socialism can be run on the basis of 'each according to his needs', since it seems that our needs will not run out until we stop making comparisons, or until we run out of objects to satisfy them – whichever comes first. (Springborg, *The Problem of Human Needs*, 110.)

56 Cohen, *Marx's Theory of History*, 307.

57 I have concentrated on the problem of material needs as formulated by Marx. Elster, *Making Sense of Marx*, 70-1, notes the problems entailed in Marx's theory of spiritual needs. These problems include those of conflicting needs and limited personal

capacities, as well as the scarcity of time that would remain. On this last point, compare Peter Stillman, "Scarcity, sufficiency, and abundance: Hegel and Marx on material needs and satisfactions," *International Political Science Review* 4, no. 3 (1983): 295-310.

58 See Herbert Marcuse, *Eros and Civilization: A Philosophical Inquiry into Freud* (Boston: Beacon Press, 1966), 151-8.

59 Thomas Carlyle, *Past and Present* (London: J. M. Dent & Sons, 1912), 1.

60 Carlyle, *Past and Present*, 5.

61 Carlyle, *Past and Present*, 139-54. For a discussion of Carlyle's critique of political economy, see Philip Rosenberg, *The Seventh Hero: Thomas Carlyle and the Theory of Radical Activism* (Cambridge, Mass.: Harvard University Press, 1974), chap. 8. Samuel Coleridge and William Blake made similar observations to Carlyle's on the paradox of poverty and plenty. See the examples cited in James Clark Sherburne, *John Ruskin, or the Ambiguities of Abundance: A Study in Social and Economic Criticism* (Cambridge, Mass.: Harvard University Press, 1972), 87-8.

62 For a good account of the Romantic sense of organicism, see Sherburne, *John Ruskin*, chap. 1.

63 In Ruskin's interpretation, Gothic architecture, alone among architectural styles, elevates the limited capacities of workers to an element of form, so that it can, "out of fragments full of imperfection, and betraying that imperfection in every touch, indulgently raise up a stately and unaccusable whole." John Ruskin, *The Works of John Ruskin*, Library Edition, ed. E.T. Cook and Alexander Wedderburn, 39 vols. (London: George Allen, 1903-12), 10:190.

64 Ruskin, *Works*, 16:18.

65. Ruskin's autobiography, *Praeterita*, does not fit the pattern of religious-conversion narrative to which Mill's *Autobiography* belongs, with its triadic structure of progress. Instead, it is noteworthy for its use of juxtapositions and interrupted narrative, a procedure that better fits his notion of history. See George P. Landow, *Ruskin* (Oxford: Oxford University Press, 1985), 73-86.

66 The St. George's Guild was Ruskin's failed project for the

establishment of communities of agricultural labor and an associated museum of art and literature for workers. See Joan Abse, *John Ruskin: The Passionate Moralist* (New York: Alfred A. Knopf, 1981), 240-4, 272-9, 298-300.

3

Economizing

The false promise of abundance held out by the belief in progress has the effect of historicizing the condition of scarcity even as it helps to sustain it. Whether envisioned in the terms of Mill's modest stationary state or Marx's more affluent true communism, the possibility of freedom from scarcity in the future makes the scarcity experienced in the present and past appear as a historical episode, albeit a necessary one. When seen from Ruskin's antiprogressive Romantic perspective, the present society of scarcity is a perverse historical curiosity, a delirious interlude of collective hubris from which we might, through an act of will, free ourselves at any moment.

All of these constructions are essentially moral in their intention, attempts to resolve the paradox of affluence. In this regard, they are continuous with the theories of Smith, Hume, and Rousseau – whether endorsing or criticizing the status quo, they, too, took the high moral ground. But by the end of the nineteenth century a different approach to the experience of scarcity had taken shape, one which restored it to the dehistoricized position it had been left in by Smith and Hume. This was accomplished in the name of science and with the intention of eliminating metaphysics from the study of human economy. It took shape within debates over the extent and content of economic theory and emerged in the triumph of neoclassical economics over the descendants of classical political economy.

*

More or less simultaneously, but independently, William Stanley Jevons in England, Leon Walras in Switzerland, and Carl Menger in Austria developed the basic groundwork for marginal utility theory, the lynchpin of the new economic science. At the center of this theory lies what has come to be known as the scarcity postulate, an assumption of the universality of the condition of scarcity that at once gives neoclassical economics its focus and provides the legitimacy of its claim to science. Fifty years after its inception, Lionel Robbins summarized this claim in a passage I have already cited in the introductory chapter, above, but which bears repeating here for its conciseness and influence:

> We have been turned out of Paradise. We have neither eternal life nor unlimited means of gratification. Everywhere we turn, if we choose one thing we must relinquish others which, in different circumstances, we would not wish to have relinquished. Scarcity of means to satisfy given ends is an almost ubiquitous condition of human behavior. Here, then, is the unity of the subject of Economic Science, the forms assumed by human behavior in disposing of scarce means.[1]

With the development of neoclassical economics, "scarcity" now became a technical concept, and a logic of scarcity – a form of rationality as universal as the condition of scarcity was deemed to be – was born.

Menger's formulation of the scarcity postulate in his *Principles of Economics* (1871) is a particularly clear statement of this logic. The starting point here, as with marginal utility theory generally, is with the assumption that human activity is directed toward the satisfaction of need. The ability to determine relationships of cause and effect is deemed to be characteristic of human beings, and progress in the area of need satisfaction is held to consist in an increase in ability to apply cause and effect calculations to the problem of satisfying needs, anticipating the chain of events that will produce the goods necessary to such satisfaction. Additionally, Menger also relies upon a Utilitarian calculation that all needs are not experienced with equal intensity by all people and that needs are capable of degrees of satisfaction. Added to this is the assumption that for most kinds of goods, within a given time period, there will be an insufficiency in quantity to satisfy all needs for that good. Menger summarizes the net result of these "insights" on the part of individuals in what amounts to a definition of marginal utility:

> men endeavor, in provident activity directed to the satisfaction of their needs . . . to make a choice between their more important needs, which they will satisfy with the available quantity of the good in question, and needs that they must leave unsatisfied, and. . .to obtain the greatest possible result with a given quantity of the good or a given result with the smallest possible quantity – or in other words to direct the quantities of consumers' goods available to them, and particularly the available quantities of the means of production, to the satisfaction of their needs in the most appropriate manner.[2]

This type of choice – essentially a calculation – and the activities it engenders, "is called economizing, and goods standing in the quantitative relationship involved in the preceding discussion [i.e., exist in insufficient supply to satisfy the need for them] are the exclusive objects of it. These goods are *economic* goods in contrast to such goods as men find no practical necessity of economizing."[3] Thus economics is solely concerned with scarce goods and the economizing actions of the individuals who need them.

By systematizing the postulate of scarcity in this way, neoclassical economics discovered what the eighteenth century had invented: a universal condition of scarcity.[4] Like their eighteenth-century predecessors, the marginalists based their conception of scarcity in a particular experience of need, one in which needs are characterized by a restless quality. Alfred Marshall's explanation of marginal utility in his *Principles of Economics* (1890) captures that quality particularly well:

> It is an almost universal law that each several want is limited, and that with every increase in the amount of a thing which a man has, the eagerness of his desire to obtain more of it diminishes; until it yields place to the desire for some other thing, of which perhaps he had hardly thought, so long as his more urgent wants were still unsatisfied. There is an endless variety of wants, but there is a limit to each separate want.[5]

In a sense, the infinite multiplicity of wants with which individuals are endowed is thought to serve as a limitation on each particular need. Because individuals have an inexhaustible fund of "wants," they impose a limit on any particular one the moment some other, relatively neglected want emerges as a contender for scarce means of satisfaction. Thus marginal utility theory can have it both ways: needs in the aggregate are infinitely expandable, but economizing individuals are continuously engaged in allocative acts that involve limitations on particular needs, rendering them calculable.[6] It is the movement from need to need that simultaneously provides for conditions of relative satiety and absolute scarcity – needs are satisfied only as long as there are other, unsatisfied ones to which the individual can turn. Individuals decide that they have had enough of one thing only at the same moment as they decide that they want something else even more. Desire – restless, perpetually unfulfilled – underlies the marginalist notion of need.

Neoclassical theory thus recreates the notion of need as desire that we found in the writings of Smith and Hume, but it does so in a desocialized manner. The earlier version had been constituted within a broader conception of the history of civil society, one in which the human characteristic of seeking ever greater refinement in useful things serves as a motor for the development of civil (as opposed to rude) society. The collapse of need into desire is accomplished through the notion that emulation first triggers and then sustains the individual's innate interest in refinement by presenting her or him with new and more refined objects of desire, and hence with new and more refined models of social status. It is therefore impossible to separate the individual and the social in any discussion of need within this discourse. But the neoclassical conception of need is presented as thoroughly individual in origin: it is constructed solely out of the individual's preferences, without any trace of social determination.[7] Marginal utility theory is deliberately unconcerned with the sources of the individual's desires (it stipulates only that such desires exist as empirical fact) or with the process by which people order them (it stipulates only that they do order them). And of course it makes no judgment on those desires of the sort that led Smith to express regret over the trinkets people covet, even if coveting them did serve a useful purpose. For the marginalists, the only issue of any relevance is the fact that a good has entered the realm of the economic because an individual wants it, or wants more of it, and expresses that want.

In part, these differences in interpretation of need are expressions of the neoclassical scientific project and the ways in which it differs from the political economy that derived from Smith's initial concern with moral philosophy. The marginalists sought to expunge metaphysical substances and contingent historical episodes from their theory. Menger, for example, rails against the idea that a thing might embody value independently of its economic status as a scarce good, as in the labor theory of value.[8] He also goes out of his way to reject any notion that the morality of rent and interest is of any concern to the science of economics.[9] These efforts are reflective of a change in subject matter: whereas classical political economy had taken wealth as its subject, neoclassical economics focuses on economizing actions, beginning with individual ones and then aggregating them. The older concern with wealth – with the production and distribution of commodities of all sorts – had given rise to all sorts of disputes over how wealth was to be understood, providing the likes of J.S. Mill, Karl Marx, and John Ruskin with a common ground for disagreement. That disagreement was more than theoretical, since the various struggles between and among the new working class, artisans, and the owners of capital revolved around ethical attitudes arising from it. The new orientation would avoid these disputes by avoiding the philosophical and historical issues – such as custom – that go into the (necessarily) social definition of wealth, as well as avoid, along the way, the question whether an abundance of wealth could be achieved. Menger expresses the change when he claims that "the end of economy is not the physical augmentation of goods but always the fullest possible satisfaction of human needs."[10] Economics would take needs as given and then study the ways individuals seek to maximize their satisfaction of them. By doing so, it would also achieve a level of universality befitting an enterprise with scientific intent.

This universality is established in two senses. First, although neoclassical economics appears to restrict its science by limiting it to scarcity situations, it expects, in Menger's version, that more and more goods will enter the realm of scarcity (and hence become economic) through a constant growth in human needs.[11] As civilization advances, therefore, scarcity situations will become generalized, and along with it the applicability of economic science. Second, by treating all situations in which needs exceed supply as scarcity situations, neoclassical economics assumes that all these situations are comparable and subject to analysis according to the same calculative logic. That is to say, there is an assumption about human nature and human reason built into the foundation of neoclassical economics, an assumption that at some deep level individuals experience the world and react to it in the same way. In this manner, economics can be established universally as a discourse applicable to any society at any time, so long as a scarcity situation can be determined.

Neoclassical economics does more than universalize a particular set of circumstances and a particular model of the rationality appropriate to it. It also universalizes a particular set of institutions – property and markets – which are deemed to be natural results of scarcity. Once again, Menger's argument is a sure guide. If human activity is directed toward the satisfaction of need over time, and if the experience that frames that activity is of an insufficiency of goods to immediately satisfy all of the individual's needs at once, then individuals will seek to appropriate the means to satisfy their needs in the future. That appropriation is property, which, along with the legal order that ensures it, can thus be seen to be entailed in the very idea of an economic good.[12] Goods that are available in relative abundance are not made into objects of property, Menger observes:

> for men are communists whenever possible under existing natural conditions. . . . In virgin forests, everyone fetches unhindered the quantity of timber he needs. . . . Thus communism is as naturally founded upon a non-economic relationship as property is founded upon one that is economic.[13]

Of course, that timber will become property as soon as the demand for it begins to impinge upon the supply, and, in the normal course of affairs, it will.

The second institutional consequence of scarcity derives from the requirement to exchange goods in order to maximize the satisfaction of needs. Adam Smith had theorized a "propensity to truck, barter and exchange, one thing for another," grounded in human nature, as an explanation for the origin of the division of labor.[14] It is that natural disposition, he argued, that allows individuals to develop particular talents, such specializations explaining how the division of labor enables the species to augment its collective productive capacity. Without this propensity,

> every man must have procured to himself every necessary and conveniency of life which he wanted. All must have had the same duties to perform, and the same work to do, and there could have been no such difference of employment as could alone give occasion to any great difference of talents.[15]

Since Smith's concern was with the production of wealth in terms of the production of goods, he focused on the question of labor, and the origins of exchange arose as a subsidiary part of that question. Menger, by contrast, is concerned with the issue of maximizing satisfaction, so he looks for the natural foundation of exchange not in terms of labor or of natural propensities, but rather in the calculation people make, in a context of scarcity and individual property, that they would rather have something that someone else has than all or part of something in their own possession. If people exchanged out of a natural propensity, Menger reasons, they would do it all the time, whereas in fact they do it only when they believe that there is something to be gained from it, namely, greater satisfaction of need.[16] In complex societies, these exchanges, when they occur, will take place in monetized markets, where the translation between goods and needs is most easily accomplished. So markets emerge out of the requirements of individuals in scarcity situations.

This last claim of neoclassical economic theory is of particular importance. Markets are crucial to the enterprise because in them economizing individuals are able to express their desires and because it is there that we can see, and measure, that expression. As Marshall observes, "the desirability or utility of a thing to a person is commonly measured by the money price that he will pay for it."[17] The consumption patterns of individuals can readily be plotted mathematically via the movement of prices, which enhances the scientific possibilities of determining the marginal utility of any particular want – needs can be quantified and approached objectively.[18] But Marshall's casual observation reveals that markets, which marginal utility theory takes to be a response to scarcity situations, are actually presupposed in the formulation of the economizing individual. Utility is "commonly" measured by prices paid because the economic actors Marshall, Menger, et al., encounter in their daily experience are already acting in market societies.

The market presupposition can be seen in the very formulation of the economizing individual. This conceptualization requires, first, that individuals experience desire for things that they do not have but that are in the possession of others and, second, that individuals will store up – "economize" – goods that they do not want in order to effect an exchange later for what they do want (or want more). That sort of calculation could only take place where markets are already institutionalized. It is not possible to derive markets from the anticipation of an exchange, but it is possible to take exchange for granted, to anticipate it, where property and markets already exist.[19] That anticipation is preceded by an acquisition of desire that the marginalists present as given but which can be seen to be external to the individual in its origin. Neoclassical theory assumes that the individual responds to wants with an economizing rationality that leads him or her to propose exchange, but the formulation of the theory suggests that it is because those wants are produced in a situation of property and exchange that the individual must economize in order to satisfy them. The difference is crucial because if the second explanation is correct, then neoclassicism's universalist claims are undermined and the scarcity postulate could be understood as valid, if valid at all, only in conditions where private property and markets are the prevailing context for the articulation and satisfaction of needs.

Indeed, it can be argued that markets help to constitute the experience of scarcity in modernity. One way in which they do this is implicit in the effect an extensively developed money-exchange system has on choice. Money plays the role of the great equalizer in market societies; money is a linguistic system in which qualitatively different things can be expressed in quantitative terms and thereby brought into a common social discourse.[20] Within such a system, a complex calculation of choices is made possible and the range of potential objects of appropriation is rendered limitless, at least in theory. In practice, social norms, ethical or religious strictures, tradition, and legal codes constrain, to some extent, the range of things that can be quantified in this way and made subject to exchange – we cannot choose to purchase a human being as a slave, for example, nor would we care to place a price tag on friendship. But a fully instituted money-exchange system expands the range of possible calculations to an almost infinite degree as compared with societies with no, or less developed, monetized systems of exchange. Thus we can and often do see a great many things in terms of their price and therefore marked as possible objects of appropriation. Because we possess a certain amount of money, or goods that can be converted into money, we experience situations of choice with regard to those things. Of course, the more money we have, the greater our power to convert things into possessions, and therefore the greater our realm of choice (or effective demand, in the economists' parlance). The indifference shown by Menger or Marshall to the specific wants of individuals is an expression of the indifference displayed by market systems to the specific quality of goods – diamonds or hot dogs, everything has its price, everything can be expressed in a common language.

The representation of things in quantitative terms means that the ends toward which needs are directed and the means by which those ends are obtained are situated on a continuum along which they can be compared and calculations of desire made.[21] The neoclassical image of an economizing individual allocating limited means among competing ends is drawn against an unacknowledged background of this peculiar sort of exchange system. On its unified terrain the world is experienced as a world of choice, a world in which everything is potentially to be had, but only a little bit at a time, and thus as a world of perpetual desire and, necessarily, perpetual frustration.

Another way to look at the contribution made by markets to the experience of scarcity is to concentrate on their character as supply and demand mechanisms. Neoclassical theory sees markets as logical responses to scarcity situations but they can also be seen as institutionalizations of such situations. Markets depend on imbalances of supply and demand in order to function, with prices acting as the mediator between existing supply and effective demand (the price necessary to clear the market). In the normal course of affairs, this leads market actors to seek to manipulate supply and demand situations in order to ensure the proper functioning of markets. These manipulations range from the deliberate restriction of supply (subsidies to farmers not to grow certain crops; import restrictions; etc.) to deliberate stimulation of demand (advertising; "planned obsolescence"; the promotion of fashion; etc.). In extreme cases, as Amartya K. Sen has shown in a study of some twentieth-century famines provoked not by gross unavailability of food but rather by the effects of markets on production and distribution,[22] these practices can lead to tragic consequences.

Living in societies in which there were highly developed market systems, it is perhaps easy to see why nineteenth-century theorists would equate economic activity in general with the specific type of activity characteristic of such systems. Economic historian Karl Polanyi distinguishes between a "substantive" sense of the term economic, in which it refers to any given set of institutions resulting from the process of material want satisfaction, and a "formal" sense, which is roughly equivalent to the Mengerian definition of economics as involving economizing actions.[23] In Polanyi's interpretation, the scarcity postulate at the center of neoclassical theory is a product of a historically contingent convergence of these two meanings:

> The last two centuries produced in Western Europe and North America an organization of man's livelihood to which the rules of choice happened to be singularly applicable. This form of the economy consisted in a system of price-making markets. Since acts of exchange, as practiced under such a system, involve the participants in choice induced by an insufficiency of means, the system could be reduced to a pattern that lent itself to the application of methods based on the formal meaning of "economic." As long as the economy was controlled by such a system, the formal and the substantivist meanings would in practice coincide.[24]

This coincidence resulted in the notion that the scarcity experienced in modernity is a universal condition experienced everywhere and at all times.

*

The universalization of the economizing individual operating in a context of markets to maximize his or her needs satisfaction that is at the core of marginalism did not go unchallenged at its inception. Both on the Continent and in Britain there were those who argued that it is an error to suppose that economic motivations are the same everywhere and at all times, asserting instead that political economy has to be comparative and historical in its focus.[25] Initially taking aim at what they perceived to be the errors of an excessively deductive approach to political economy, principally in its Ricardian form, these so-called historical schools maintained that the institutions of a commercial society and the patterns of behavior they encourage and express are unique to modern commercial society.[26] They attacked the abstractness of marginalism and accused it of an abrogation of the moral and political responsibility of economic analysis, an attack that was often contained, in England, within the broader assault on *laissez-faire* doctrine.

    In the end, marginalism prevailed as the new orthodoxy, political economy became economics, and the historical economists unwittingly wound up establishing the new field of economic history. The story of this episode is as much one of academic politics as of anything else, a story told, from the viewpoint of the losers, in Alon Kadish's study, *The Oxford Economists in the Late Nineteenth Century*. But marginalism's success carried economics beyond the areas of academic departments and public policy, and that success owes a great deal to its ability to simplify and systematize an experience and a process of reasoning common to people living in a modern society.

Economizing reason is essentially a process of relating means to ends. The ends themselves are taken as given and lie outside of the process of economic reasoning. Max Weber classed the kind of activity that embodies this form of reason as a subset of "instrument-ally rational (*zweckrational*)" action in his typology of social action. Contrasted with "value rational (*wertrational*)" action, which is oriented toward specific substantive ends, instrumentally rational action is concerned with calculating efficient means. The ends themselves may be determined in a value rational way, or, as in economic rationality,

> the actor may, instead of deciding between alternative and conflicting ends in terms of a rational orientation to a system of values, simply take them as given subjective wants and arrange them in a scale of consciously assessed relative urgency. He may then orient his action to this scale in such a way that they are satisfied as far as possible in order of urgency, as formulated in the principle of "marginal utility."

Weber adds that from the point of view of instrumentally rational action, "value rationality is always irrational."[27]

Weber's characterizations of rationality are instructive because they bring out central features of the economizing rationality we have been discussing. Within the structure of value rationality, to choose between two ends is a moral, ethical, or political problem that can be governed by considerations of custom, tradition, religion, social solidarity, etc. The subject of the act looks to some value system in order to choose, though in some instances – perhaps even in most – the choice may be foreclosed by that system, and then justifies the choice to self or others on that basis. Within the structure of instrumental, or economizing rationality, none of these consider-ations are of any importance. Ends are ordered according to subjective preference on the basis of the relative strength of the desires felt for them. To extend Weber's point, acting in this way can only be perceived as irrational from a value rational perspective, since no judgment of the ends as ends takes place. Whereas value rationality focuses on the qualitative character of the ends to be considered, instrumental rationality treats all ends as points on the continuum of desire. A moral choice between two objects may very well decide the matter once and for all, and so the choice is absolute. An economizing choice only entails a particular choice at a particular time, since, having decided that one object will give greater satisfaction to desire than another or others, a person may find that the spurned choice, or one of them, now presents itself as a newly powerful want, and so it becomes the preferred object of acquisition in the future. Thus value rationality may set absolute limits on the range of choices with which the subject may be confronted, while instrumental rationality implies the existence of no such limit.

As Weber noted, to choose between ends on the basis of some value system is irrational from the point of view of instrumental reason, which is to say that the terms of such a choice lie outside its calculative logic. The only rational choice for an economizing individual is the most efficient one. While it is possible to structure a situation so that ends are chosen on value rational grounds and then pursued in an instrumentally rational way, economizing rationality has no need for value rationality, since the tenets of marginal utility can establish ends on its own grounds. So economic rationality can be distinguished from the broader category of instrumental rationality insofar as it is one form of instrumental reason that can generate its own ends and is therefore potentially independent of value rationality altogether.

This characteristic is of utmost importance when it is recalled that economizing rationality is born out of and thrives in situations of monetized calculation.[28] The growth of a market system, with its expansion into areas of social life whose constitutive principles had hitherto been found in custom, religion, tradition, etc., expands the potential reach of its distinctive rationality to the exclusion of value rational competitors. As those competitors fall, so do the possible limits to the ends people pursue. A dynamic is created in which those ends are transformed from qualitatively different ends to quantitatively similar ones, and so the area of human choice is reconstituted as a continuum of desire. Instrumental rationality, particularly in its economizing form, can then be expected gradually to become dominant over substantive rationality as the effort to choose between ends on substantive grounds is increasingly seen as irrational.

Weber expressed something of this dynamic in his interpretation of the development of western market society in *The Protestant Ethic and the Spirit of Capitalism* (1904-5). The Calvinist, Weber thought, felt called to a worldly aestheticism, an economizing vocation, wherein rational calculation served the higher purpose of God's will. But the pursuit of wealth comes to undermine that and other higher purposes as its distinctive rationality pushes faith out of the way. The forces of material desire are unleashed and in the modern world, "the idea of duty in one's calling prowls about in our lives like the ghost of dead religious beliefs."[29]

Those irrational ghosts notwithstanding, instrumental reason comes close to having the field to itself. Even Weber gave in to the temptation to associate it with scientific rationality and so, with a very short leap in usage, to equate it with rationality as such. It is the calculability that is built into instrumental rationality that facilitates this slippage. The growth of rationality in the modern world

> means that principally there are no mysterious incalculable forces that come into play, but rather that one can, on principle, master all things by calculation. This means that the world is disenchanted. One need no longer have recourse to magical means in order to master or implore the spirits, as did the savage, for whom such mysterious powers existed. Technical means and calculations perform the service. This above all is what intellectualization means.[30]

But this "disenchantment" also means that substantive social ends become difficult to formulate – they increasingly appear as irrationally held beliefs. The ability to choose an efficient course of action is enhanced, but the ability to choose the end toward which that action should be directed is circumscribed. By contrast, individual wants, easily formulated in calculable terms, take on a central importance, eventually substituting, in the aggregate, for substantive social goals.

What results from this development is a social environment in which the realm of choice is constantly expanding, thus expanding the experience of scarcity. That experience, in turn, reinforces the truth claims of economizing rationality. The calculating logic of scarcity takes on the character of common sense. In its crude form, this sense is displayed in the "time is money" homilies of Ben Franklin that so interested Max Weber. Today it is universalized in the more sophisticated vocabulary of cost-benefit analysis.

*

The economizing individual at the center of the marginalist revolution is an abstraction. The rational individual, fully aware of all potential uses to which his or her resources can be placed in order to satisfy given wants, is a convenience. It enables economists to figure certain things out in anticipation of aggregate demand, but it ignores other features of everyday observation. In an essay published in 1909, Thorstein Veblen objected that marginal utility theory rests on the uncritically accepted psychological premise of a "hedonistic calculus" that dictates its image of rationality. For that reason, the theory cannot explain behavior that is not oriented toward the consumption of goods. For example:

> business men habitually aspire to accumulate wealth in excess of the limits of practicable consumption, and the wealth so accumulated is not intended to be converted by a final transaction of purchase into consumable goods or sensations of consumption. Such commonplace facts as these, together with the endless web of business detail of a like pecuniary character, do not in hedonistic theory raise a question as to how these conventional aims, ideals, aspirations, and standards have come into force or how they affect the scheme of life in business outside of it; they do not raise those questions because such questions cannot be answered in the terms which the hedonistic economists are content to use, or, indeed, which their premises permit them to use.[31]

From the marginalist's point of view, the sorts of phenomena we associate with Veblen's name (but which, as we saw in Chapter 1, above, were formulated earlier, in the eighteenth century), such as conspicuous consumption and pecuniary emulation, are instances of what we might call counterintuitive behavior. The rational economizer does not adjust his or her desire for some object upward with an increase in price for that object, but a consumer acting in the context of prestige display and emulative acquisition does.[32] Veblen's criticism comes down to acknowledging that marginalism's indifference to the process by which desires are acquired, in favor of concentrating on a hypothetical individual with given wants, blinds it to forms of social rationality that dictate what consumers actually do, rather than what an economic rationalizer is supposed to do.

The fact that a monetized market economy renders an otherwise impossibly large number of goods quantitatively comparable and therefore transforms them into potential objects of appropriation does not mean that these objects become altogether devoid of qualitative characteristics. What it does mean is that the utility of goods becomes secondary to the value that they come to have as elements within a symbolic order of consumption. That order, to which we turn in the next chapter, obeys a logic that is at odds with the economizing logic of a universe of scarcity.

NOTES

1   Lionel Robbins, *The Nature and Significance of Economic Science* (London: Macmillan, 1932), 15.
2   Carl Menger, *Principles of Economics*, trans. James Dingwall and Bert F. Hoselitz (New York and London: New York University Press, 1981), 95-6.
3   Menger, *Principles*, 96.
4   Eric Roll, *A History of Economic Thought* (London: Faber and Faber, 1961), 387, notes, with reference to Menger's classification of goods as either economic or noneconomic, that

> when they are in the economic class, goods may be said to possess 'scarcity', a term which earlier English writers had never fully assimilated into the system. August Walras, the father of Leon, had used *rareté* in something like the Mengerian sense. But Menger was the first, without using the word, to express precisely this quantitative relation between ends and means to which the word is now applied.

5   Alfred Marshall, *Principles of Economics* (London: Macmillan, 1890), 155.
6   Menger, *Principles*, 82-3, adds that economics and economizing actions deal with finite periods of time, thus limiting potentially infinite needs. Were it not for these stipulations, of course, the infinity of needs presupposed by marginalist theory would render impossible the attempt to measure them.

7   See David P. Levine, *Economic Studies: Contributions to the Critique of Economic Theory* (London: Routledge & Kegan Paul, 1977), 181.
8   Menger, *Principles*, 102.
9   Menger, *Principles*, 173:

> One of the strangest questions ever made the subject of scientific debate is whether rent and interest are justified from an ethical point of view or whether they are 'immoral.' Among other things, our science has the task of exploring why and under what conditions the services of land and of capital display economic character, attain value, and can be exchanged for quantities of other economic goods (prices). But it seems to me that the question of the legal or moral character of these facts is beyond the sphere of our science.

10   Menger, *Principles*, 190.
11   Menger, *Principles*, 103: "with advancing civilization non-economic goods show a tendency to take on economic character, chiefly because one of the factors involved is the magnitude of human requirements, which increase with the progressive development of civilization,"
12   Menger, *Principles*, 97:

> Thus human economy and property have a joint economic origin since both have, as the ultimate reason for their existence, the fact that goods exist whose available quantities are smaller than the requirements of men. Property, therefore, like human economy, is not an arbitrary invention but rather the only practically possible solution of the problem that is, in the nature of things, imposed upon us by the disparity between requirements for, and available quantities of, all economic goods.

13   Menger, *Principles*, 100-1.
14   Adam Smith, *An Inquiry into the Nature and Causes of the Wealth of Nations*, ed. R.H. Campbell, A.S. Skinner and W.B. Todd, 2 vols. (Oxford: Clarendon Press, 1976), 1:25.
15   Smith, *Wealth of Nations*, 1:29.
16   Menger, *Principles*, 175-80.
17   Marshall, *Principles*, 151.
18   The possibility of presenting mathematical formulations for economic explanation is intrinsic to the marginalist theory, even

when presented in a nonmathematical way. The point was made
with regard to Menger by John Neville Keynes, *The Scope and
Method of Political Economy*, 4th edn (London: Macmillan,
1917), 266n: "It may be said that the work of Menger and his
followers is mathematical in tone, though not in language." But
see Mark Blaug, *Economic Theory in Retrospect*, 4th edn
(Cambridge: Cambridge University Press, 1985), 296, where the
Austrian school's nonmathematical approach is emphasized.

19 See Levine, *Economic Studies*, 184-5.
20 See Helen Codere, "Money-exchange systems and a theory of
money," *Man* 3, no. 4 (1968): 557-77. For a discussion undertaken within a Marxist framework, see W. F. Haug, *Critique of
Commodity Aesthetics: Appearance, Sexuality and Advertising
in Capitalist Society*, trans. Robert Bock (Minneapolis: University of Minnesota Press, 1986), chap. 1.
21 Levine, *Economic Studies*, 294-5.
22 Amartya K. Sen, *Poverty and Famines: An Essay on Entitle-
ments and Deprivation* (Oxford: Clarendon Press, 1982).
23 Karl Polanyi, "The economy as instituted process," in Karl
Polanyi, Conrad M. Arensberg, and Harry W. Pearson, eds., *Trade
and Markets in the Early Empires* (Chicago: Gateway Edition,
1971), 243. Elsewhere, Polanyi claims that Menger noted this
distinction in the posthumously published, and untranslated,
second edition of his *Principles* (1923), where he introduced the
substantivist meaning of economic. See Karl Polanyi, "Carl
Menger's two meanings of 'economic'," in *Studies in Economic
Anthropology*, ed. George Dalton (Washington, D.C.: American
Anthropological Association, 1971), 16-24.
24 Polanyi, "The economy as instituted process," 244.
25 For a discussion of the controversies between the historical and
analytic schools in Austria and Germany, see T. W. Hutchison, *A
Review of Economic Doctrines, 1870-1929* (Oxford: Clarendon
Press, 1953), 130-96. For the English story, see A. W. Coats, "The
historicist reaction in English political economy, 1870-90,"
Economica, n.s. 21 (1954): 143-53; Gerard M. Koot, "English
historical economics and the emergence of economic history in
England," *History of Political Economy* 12 (1980): 174-205; Alon
Kadish, *The Oxford Economists in the Late Nineteenth Century*
(Oxford: Clarendon Press, 1982); Stefan Collini, Donald Winch,
and John Burrow, *That Noble Science of Politics: A Study in*

Nineteenth-Century Intellectual History (Cambridge: Cambridge University Press, 1983), chap. 8. Although the English historicists made use of arguments developed by the German historical school, the two movements arose independently.

26 Similar positions were taken by some who were not associated with the historical school, *per se*. Walter Bagehot, for example, argued that political economy should be seen as a theory dealing with the causes of wealth "in a single kind of society – a society of grown-up competitive commerce such as we have in England." Quoted in Collini, et al., *That Noble Science of Politics*, 256.

27 Max Weber, *Economy and Society: An Outline of Interpretive Sociology*, trans. Guenther Roth and Claus Wittich (Berkeley and Los Angeles: University of California Press, 1978), 26.

28 Weber, *Economy and Society*, 85, notes that "a system of economic activity will be called 'formally' rational according to the degree in which the provision for needs, which is esssential to every rational economy, is capable of being expressed in numerical, calculable terms, and is so expressed."

29 Max Weber, *The Protestant Ethic and the Spirit of Capitalism* (New York: Scribner's, 1958), 182.

30 Max Weber, "Science as a vocation," in *From Max Weber: Essays in Sociology*, ed. H.H. Gerth and C. Wright Mills (New York: Oxford University Press, 1958), 139.

31 Thorstein Veblen, "The limitation of marginal utility," in *The Place of Science in Modern Civilization and Other Essays* (New York: Russell & Russell, 1961), 249.

32 Economic theory has, of course, attempted to integrate such behavior into its theoretical system at an aggregate level. See, for example, H. Leibenstein, "Bandwagon, snob, and Veblen effects in the theory of consumers' demand," *Quarterly Journal of Economics* 64 (1950): 183-207.

4

Consuming

The discourse of scarcity and abundance that marks the nineteenth century accompanied the creation of an environment carefully crafted to elicit sensations of opulence and desire. The essence of this environment, which is still ours, consists of sight and movement. The eighteenth-century invention of bowed shop windows that intruded on the sidewalk, virtually forcing their attention on passers-by, appears crude when compared to the arcades, commercial expositions, and department stores that followed, each of them adding another element of display to the quotidian experience of hurrying, strolling, or meandering crowds. The use of electricity for light and power set the backdrop of things in motion as well, even before the advent of cinema and television, creating an integrated world of illumination and animation.

Paris, the capital of civilization and of shopping, was a pioneering city in this process of environmental transfiguration. Walter Benjamin deployed the Marxist category of commodity fetishism to evoke this environment in his series of sketches written in 1935, "Paris, capital of the nineteenth century," an unpublished part of his unfinished "Arcades Project."[1] Enclosed passageways lined with shops that cut through blocks of buildings and connected streets, the arcades began appearing in Paris around 1800, though they proliferated in the period from 1820 to 1840.[2] Construction began for the first building specifically designed as a department store, the Bon Marché, in 1869. World expositions (modeled on the Crystal Palace exhibition of 1851) were held in Paris in 1855, 1867, 1878, 1889, and 1900. Benjamin sees all of these phenomena as spatial evidence that people have become enchanted by things. The world expositions, vast carnivals of commerce, industry, and progress, are "places of pilgrimage to the fetish Commodity." Once at that site, the pilgrims enter into a phantasmagorical world of motion and of artifice in which people and things are intermingled. Combining pragmatism and fantasy, each of the expositions included a Galerie des Machines, displaying state of the art industrial machinery, and exotic representations of the sights and temptations of far-off places.[3] Linking these extremes were the displays of clothing, furniture, and other consumer goods, which partook of the color and tactile qualities of the exotic while providing evidence of the promise and reward of industrialization. Throughout, there was movement and simulation, from the moving parts of the Galeries des Machines to the undulations of belly dancers on the "Rue du Caire" (at the 1889 exhibition), from the tumble and hues of fabric to panoramas, dioramas, and animated exhibits. And around it all was a steady stream of human circulation.

The vast scale of the interiors necessary for this display and movement was made possible by the use of steel and glass in construction. The arcades had been enclosed by these materials, allowing light into the passageways, but it was in the design of exhibition halls, department stores, and railroad terminals, where the circulation of great numbers of people was of paramount importance, that the real possiblities of glass and steel construction were realized. One feature of the architecture that resulted is that the interiors of these buildings were organized around central spaces open to the skylit roofs. The Grand Magasin au Bon Marché, built between 1869 and 1887, is a classic example of this feature placed at the service of a society of consumption. The Bon Marché's architect, L. A. Boileau, and engineer, Gustav Eiffel, whose famous tower was constructed for the 1889 world exhibition, designed a series of skylit interior courts that allowed the natural light thought best for displaying the store's goods into the display areas.[4] Above the ground floor of the courts, where products were laid out on display tables and counters, were series of balconies and iron bridges with open flooring that allowed for movement between courts and for the passage of light to the floor below.[5] Encased in an exterior of heavily ornamented masonry, the Bon Marché fits particularly well the general observation of an historian of Parisian architecture: "The department store was a 'people's palace,' an easily accessible center of luxury and display, where the elaborate decor provided an atmosphere conducive to enjoyment and spending."[6] But beyond the display of opulence on the tables and in the masonry, part of that enjoyable atmosphere was due as well to the ability to be able to look down from those balconies and bridges and to gaze upon the shoppers. In the Bon Marché, as at the expositions, where balconies surrounded the Galeries des Machines, people were placed on display along with the commodities.[7]

The display of persons and things was part of the department store's ambience, and it was something new. Previously, shopping had been an altogether different, and rather solitary, experience. The innovations in retailing that were characteristic of London in the eighteenth century were slow to take hold in Paris. There, advertising was virtually unknown until the 1830s, around the same time that shops began to mark fixed prices on goods. Haggling had been the standard practice, with customers more or less obligated to make a purchase once they entered a store but with no similar obligation on the part of proprietors to be pleasant or honest in return.[8] Fixed prices, open entry to the store, courteous clerks, and policies allowing returns were some of the new amenities offered by the *magasins de nouveautés* (drapery and fancy goods stores) that lined the arcades. These stores, and the department stores, or *grands magasins*, that emerged from them, allowed unfettered access to great varieties of goods, and thus virtually invented the modern pastime of browsing.

The new retailing establishments became a kind of institutionalized fair or permanent world exhibition. The point of their displays was not necessarily the sale of any particular item, although all were potential objects of appropriation. The point was the atmosphere itself. "As environments of mass consumption," Rosalind Williams writes, "department stores were, and still are, places where consumers are an audience to be entertained by commodities, where selling is mingled with amusement, where arousal of free-floating desire is as important as immediate purchase of particular items."[9] That desire is aroused in part through the display of opulence – oriental rugs draped over department store railings were a favorite sign of exotic wealth – but depends, in the last resort, on the creation of a style (or styles) to which consumption is subordinated. In chapter 1, we saw how eighteenth-century English entrepreneurs manipulated fashion and social esteem in order to create a market for goods whose value depended upon their qualities as signs of social rank rather than as specific items of utility. By the time of the department stores, retailers were able to bring not only improvements in architectural technology to bear on expanding this strategy, but also had more efficient and far-reaching communications and transportation net-works available. One such resource was in mail-order catalogues. While London merchants relied primarily on the seasonal flow of fashionable individuals between their town and country homes, the French department stores used catalogue mailings to sell directly to provincials. The Bon Marché mailed out 1.5 million illustrated catalogues during the winter of 1894 alone, about half of which went to the provinces, while some 260,000 were sent abroad.[10] Mail order sales were a profitable part of the store's business, but the catalogues also sold an image of Parisian fashion that helped to shape conceptions of desirable and acceptable styles in clothing, home furnishings, recreation, and, at a less overt level, proper behavior.[11]

*

The number of locations for viewing and comparing one another with regard to fashion expanded greatly during the nineteenth century. In addition to department stores and world expositions, first the arcades and later the boulevards of Paris provided the spaces for strolling and observing. The boulevards, the broad, linear avenues that we think of as quintessentially Parisian, were largely the result of Louis Napoleon's project for the rebuilding of Paris, under the direction of Baron Haussmann, that began in the 1850s. The narrow, densely packed streets of the old Paris gave way to these boulevards, which in turn made possible the development of a mass transportation system in the city that facilitated the success of the department stores, allowing customers to venture out of their *quartiers*.[12] Another benefit of the boulevards was of more immediate importance to Louis Napoleon in the wake of the 1848 revolution: the broad avenues would make the erection of barricades more difficult and provide a clear line of fire for artillery. While the boulevards played their part in allowing the Parisian bourgeoisie to emerge politically victorious with the suppression of the Paris Commune of 1871, their role in the social preeminence of that class is less obvious. Access to the department stores is only a part of that story. Of more importance is the emergence of the boulevards as spaces of social display.

The arcades, offering protection from vehicular terror in Paris' narrow streets, had allowed the creation of shop windows as showcases for luxury goods and provided the opportunity for gathering and strolling, for observing and being observed:

In the time of its conception the arcade was home to luxury and fashion. It offered to the bourgeois public in all its various guises – the *flâneur*, the bohemian, the *boulevardier* – the opportunity to display itself to the world. It presented the myriad products of a blossoming luxury industry for gazing, buying, flaunting and consuming.[13]

Haussmann's redevelopment replaced the arcades with the boulevards, which took over their social role, but in a broad sense the arcades and the boulevards are of a piece. In Benjamin's recreation of nineteenth-century Paris, the arcades provided the milieu that gave birth to the *flâneur*, the characteristically French literary man in the crowd.[14] The *flâneur* is adept at reading surfaces – of things and of people – and of classifying them: he "goes botanizing on the asphalt."[15] This botanical expertise is the sensibility of the modern urbanite; the *flâneur* possesses it to an exquisite degree. It is a sensibility that arises out of the increasing opportunities afforded by urban life for viewing and being seen by others, by the anonymity afforded by crowds, and by the desire both to stand out among and to recede into those crowds. For his part, essentially an observer, the *flâneur* recedes. Baudelaire, the poet of *flânerie*, described the type in his portrayal of "The painter of modern life" (1863):

> The crowd is his domain, just as the air is the bird's, and water that of the fish. His passion and his profession is to merge with the crowd. For the perfect idler, for the passionate observer it becomes an immense source of enjoyment to establish his dwelling in the throng, in the ebb and flow, the bustle, the fleeting and the infinite. To be away from home and yet to feel at home anywhere; to see the world, to be at the very centre of the world, and yet to be unseen of the world, such are some of the minor pleasures of those independent, intense and impartial spirits, who do not lend themselves easily to linguistic definitions. The observer is a prince enjoying his incognito wherever he goes.[16]

But while the *flâneur* revels in his anonymity, his calling involves cataloguing the individual types within the crowd and therefore differentiating it.

The code that the *flâneur* deciphers, the language in which the crowd articulates itself, is that of fashion. Fashion is the essence of modernity, of "the transient, the fleeting, the contingent."[17] Fashion is the discourse of the boulevard, the sovereign signifier of status, of membership and exclusion. As we saw in chapter 1, the decline of aristocratic society ushers in a new era in which social status is cut loose from an established order of horizontally constituted, separated levels of emulation. While horizontal emulation continues to exercise a hold on status groups, it becomes overlaid by a vertical process of emulation that begins to be felt as the middle class seeks to emulate a nobility increasingly incapable of maintaining its accustomed degree of exclusive consumption. That vertical process is made possible by the growth of a single sign system of status, which is the external display of wealth embodied in things, that is legible to the entire society. In addition, those things must, in principle, be possible objects of appropriation for everyone – that is, they must be experienced as objects of desire. In post-revolutionary France, although the consumption style of the deposed aristocracy continued to function as an ideal type,[18] the ascendant bourgeoisie began the task of creating such a sign system in order to establish its own position as pretender to the throne of status arbiter. The terrain in which this system was developed shifted from the salon to the boulevard, which became an interior for an entire class, a place to show off its possessions and to assert its identity, and its internal struggles, through the shifting vagaries of fashion.

The figures in the catalogues and the customers one encountered in the stores, the boulevard strollers and patrons arriving for the opera all served as models of contemporary fashion, and in this sense the spectacular sites of nineteenth-century Paris helped to coalesce a bourgeois style. But this style was not without its internal distinctions, ranging from a self-selecting exclusivity among the upper reaches of the middle class to the newly embourgeoisified mass consumers at the bottom. In this age of the "democratization of luxury," as it was commonly claimed to be, the middle class's aping of aristocratic style was transformed – the bourgeoisie imitated itself imitating what it took to be aristocratic modes of consumption. The trend-setters, the truly fashionable set, did not shop in the department stores. Indeed, they disdained, more than ever, the attempted usurpation of their stylistic prerogatives by the mass consuming bourgeoisie. More women could afford silk dresses, which filtered down the social order to the middle classes as a sign of luxurious taste, but the cut and quality of the cloth of these ready-mades gave them away to the discerning snob. What was important was that while those above them in social standing prided themselves on their ability instantaneously to read a person's style and make the proper determination of their relative taste and the social status that followed, mass consumers were wrapped up in a fantasy of the appearance of wealth and unable to see the often subtle difference between their imitative style and its model. The department store's role was to feed that fantasy and to create a simulated "palace" for the bourgeoisie.[19]

The effort is inherently self-defeating to the extent that a disjuncture exists between the fantasy and the basis of the style of life being imitated. From the point of view of the imitator, as Adam Smith noted much earlier, what is desirable is the perceived comfort that luxury entails, while from the point of view of the imitated, what is desirable is that which differentiates oneself from others. For the latter, then, luxury signifies things that everyone does not have and cannot have: it means possession of scarce goods. By promoting a fashion for a mass consuming public, the department stores could promote the illusion of comfort, but in the long run deprived the goods they sold in such quantity of auras of luxury, which remained, then as now, the preserve of a fashionable elite.[20]

*

By the end of the nineteenth century, the social role of fashion had become a subject of considerable interest to sociologists. George Simmel turned his attention to it in an essay published in 1904, in which he connected fashion to the general problem of personal and group identity:

> Fashion is the imitation of a given example and satisfies the demand for social adaptation; it leads the individual upon the road which all travel, it furnishes a general condition, which resolves the conduct of every individual into a mere example. At the same time it satisfies in no less degree the need of differentiation, the tendency towards dissimilarity, the desire for change and contrast, on the one hand by a constant change of contents, which gives to the fashion of today an individual stamp as opposed to that of yesterday and of to-morrow, on the other hand because fashions differ for different classes – the fashions of the upper stratum of society are never identical with those of the lower; in fact they are abandoned by the former as soon as the latter prepares to appropriate them. Thus fashion represents nothing more than one

of the many forms of life by the aid of which we seek to combine in uniform spheres of activity the tendency towards social equalization with the desire for individual differentiation and change.[21]

This need simultaneously to equalize and differentiate is felt most strongly in modernity, Simmel suggests, because of the great pressures of social conformity present in the age. Fashion – in the sense of the latest fashion or avant-garde style, which is the sense Simmel gives to it – is particularly well suited to serve this double-edged role because the decline of fixed group identities leads to greater latitude for imitation, while an increase in money wealth throughout society makes fashion a prime target for such imitation. As classes get closer to each other in terms of wealth

> the more frantic becomes the desire for imitation from below and the seeking for the new from above. The increase of wealth is bound to hasten the process considerably and render it visible, because the objects of fashion, embracing as they do the externals of life, are most accessible to the mere call of money, and conformity to the higher set is more easily acquired here than in fields which demand an individual test that gold and silver cannot affect.[22]

So while it is clear that fashion, in the up-to-date, exclusionary sense, requires the constant creation of something new, in order for it to function as a means of social differentiation it must be articulated within a common set of understandings – fashion as an ongoing activity in a broader sense. There must be novelty, but it must be novelty that is recognized as a mark of fashion and that is at least potentially capable of being imitated and purchased. In this way, fashion can act at one and the same time as a force of social differentiation and cohesion.[23]

The fashionable objects that serve as signs of social inclusion and individual or group demarcation thus have no intrinsic social value of their own, their value is derived solely from their use as signs, whatever utility such objects may have is completely secondary and socially irrelevant.[24] Adam Smith had discovered this much earlier when he tried to figure out the prestige value of the novelties of his day, as we saw in chapter 1. The most famous of the investigators into fashion to emerge at the end of the nineteenth century, Thorstein Veblen, explored the sign system of fashion and prestige in

his *Theory of the Leisure Class* (1899). Like Simmel, Veblen stressed
that in modern, urban cultures, individuals routinely encounter
strangers – to whom they, in turn, are strangers – in public places and
conveyances, while drawing the consequences of these fleeting
encounters in terms of displays of social standing:

> In the modern community there is . . . a more frequent attendance
> at large gatherings of people to whom one's everyday life is
> unknown; in such places as churches, theatres, ballrooms, hotels,
> parks, shops, and the like. In order to impress these transient
> observers, and to retain one's self-complacency under their
> observation, the signature of one's pecuniary strength should be
> written in characters which he who runs may read.[25]

The characters are external signs of wealth, while fashion provides
the language within which they are formed into intelligible signs. It is
the style in which objects connotative of wealth are combined that
gives those objects their specific denotative meaning, defining their
possessor's place in the social order relative to the styles of other
persons and groups. Style can be taken in "on the run," condensing an
entire process of social differentiation into a single glance.

The styles themselves are as fleeting as the social encounters they
mediate, which is why fashion is the perfect expression of modernity.
Both Veblen and Simmel saw something destructive in the constant
change inflicting fashion. In Simmel's view, this phenomenon is
restricted to the fashion leadership of what he calls the "demi-
monde," a role that follows on "its peculiarly uprooted form of life."
Turning this uprootedness into a permanent form of social protest,
the demi-monde adopts outrageous fashions:

> In this continual striving for new, previously unheard-of fashions,
> in the regardlessness with which the one that is most diametrically
> opposed to the existing one is passionately adopted, there lurks an
> aesthetic expression of the desire for destruction, which seems to
> be an element peculiar to all that lead this pariah-like existence, so
> long as they are not completely enslaved within.[26]

But the demi-monde's rootlessness is just an extreme case of the
rootlessness of modern society, and so its fashion sense is an extreme
case of what is generally true of fashion in a social situation of
perpetual flux. Veblen interprets this aesthetic of destruction as being
fundamental to fashion's role as social signifier. He does so by

subsuming it under the more general category of conspicuous waste, a concept that conveys the insignificance of the use value of objects for their performance of prestige functions. Fashion therefore operates as a signifier of wealth in a way similar to ancient liturgies or the potlatches of northwest coastal Indians – by showing a disregard for the material quality of things in favor of the symbolic power emanating from their destruction.[27] Hence the compulsive changeful-ness of style and the purposeful disregard for bodily comfort Veblen finds to be characteristic of modern, western fashion.[28]

The waste that Veblen sees reflected in fashion is not a waste of resources in terms of social standing; indeed, it is functionally required for that purpose. This fact, the utility of the purposive destruction of wealth entailed in the struggle for social recognition, ties the modern age to previous ages, as Veblen saw. However, two aspects of conspicuous display in the bourgeois era separate our age from its predecessors. The first is the universal character such expenditures assume in a nominally egalitarian age without fixed boundaries to social status. The other is the bad conscience that exists in relation to these displays, a bad conscience that has its origins in a conflict within the logic of the accumulation of wealth. On the one hand, the modern age spawns an ethic of saving in accordance with the accumulation of wealth necessary to challenge aristocratic social domination. Often, this ethic entails the notion of a moral superiority. Such a self-conception corresponds to the one made familiar by Max Weber's influential *Protestant Ethic and the Spirit of Capitalism*. On the other hand, as Adam Smith and David Hume emphasized, conspicuous display plays an important func-tional role in generating wealth in a commercial society, spurring social emulation and inspiring everyone to accumulate wealth in order to spend it on their own display. Under such circumstances, the two imperatives – the one toward accumulation, the other toward expenditure – are bound to come into periodic conflict. As a result, the bourgeois age is never entirely comfortable with the universe of conspicuous consumption it has engendered.[29]

*

The wasteful expenditure represented by fashion points to a side of the relationship between luxury and scarcity that eludes much common observation: it is not the scarcity of certain objects that determines their status as luxury items; it is their status as luxury items that renders them scarce objects. The social underpinnings of fashion require a search for something new in order to set the fashionable apart from everyone else. Because something is scarce it does not follow that it will be desired, but the desire to distinguish oneself pushes the search for something unique. The thing's value does not lie in its scarcity, but only in the social significance its scarcity has for its possessor. More accurately, its value lies in the social signficance of its possession by the person or group that possesses it. Adobe dwellings in New Mexico were always limited in number; they became luxurious, desired objects only when certain people – movie stars and other celebrities with very public consumption patterns – began to acquire them. Their scarcity value does not derive from their finitude but only from their transformation into signifiers of status.

Fashion may also result in the reverse phenomenon. For a brief moment, an object that exists in great quantity may attain to the level of fashion when it is incorporated into a particular style that transforms it, makes it no longer ordinary. When this occurs, it makes no sense to say that the object has a scarcity value – although once the fashion has caught on there may be a temporary lack of available supply of it to satisfy an unexpected fashion demand. What does have a scarcity value is the transforming style itself: the object in its fashionable surroundings becomes scarce because only some people have the stylistic acumen to display it in this particular way. In this sense, the stylish always possess a scarce resource independently of the things themselves that they make fashionable.

The emulation that is typical of modernity and is institutionalized in fashion can be characterized as an effort not only – or not at all – to possess what others possess, but to imitate their style. In much the same way that biographies can be appealing because in them one can see whole a life that is never seen that way by the person who lives it, another person's style can be attractive because it constitutes a whole. The more natural that style appears, the less effort in construction it seems to require by its possessor, the more appealing it may be, particularly because when we think of our own style it is hard to think of what we are "naturally." Of course, this perception of the style of others can be completely misleading. For a generation of American filmgoers, Cary Grant epitomized effortless, natural style, but Cary Grant was a cinematic illusion. The illusory quality of this product was seen clearly by Grant (née Archie Leach) himself. "Everyone wants to be Cary Grant," he is reported once to have said. "Even *I* want to be Cary Grant."[30]

The prototype of the stylish persona is the dandy, whose origins lie in the nineteenth century. Baudelaire thought that, in his meticulous appearance and dedication to leisure, the dandy expressed an aristocratic element and accorded him a section of "The painter of modern life" (along with pomp and ceremony, the soldier, woman, make-up, and the courtesan) as representative of an aspect of the modern age:

> the dandy does not aspire to wealth as an object in itself; an open bank credit could suit him just as well; he leaves that squalid passion to vulgar mortals. Contrary to what a lot of thoughtless people seem to believe, dandyism is not even an excessive delight in clothes and material elegance. For the perfect dandy, these things are no more than the symbol of the aristocratic superiority of his mind. Thus, in his eyes, enamoured as he is above all of distinction, perfection in dress consists in absolute simplicity, which is, indeed, the best way of being distinguished. What then can this passion be, which has crystallized into a doctrine, and has formed a number of outstanding devotees, this unwritten code that has moulded so proud a brotherhood? It is, above all, the burning desire to create a personal form of originality, within the external limits of social conventions.[31]

The career of the first dandy characterizes the type. Seizing the opportunity provided by the loosening of social status in England during the Napoleonic Wars, Beau Brummell created himself as a new kind of aristocrat, one whose status depends entirely upon personal style.[32] That style was constituted by nuances expressed in attire and behavior. In clothing, Brummell eschewed aristocratic costume. Instead, he pushed the trend toward uniformity in men's fashion to its limits, relying on the expertness of cut and detail to convey his superior sensibility. Compared with Brummell, other men appeared badly dressed, even if their outfits were nominally identical in composition. In fact, the point was precisely that they could be compared because the outward fashion was the same – distinction in this realm is only possible on a common ground. For those who were close enough to Brummell's taste to tell the difference between their own level of stylistic accomplishment and his, the feeling of being inadequately turned out was personally devastating. But these underachievers could at least join with Brummell in the knowing, silent ridicule of the unfortunates who mistakenly thought they were successfully aping the paragon of good taste.

As a complement to the elegant austerity of his clothing, Brummell affected an austerity of demeanor that appeared equally natural even if it was equally studied. The indifference in the gaze Brummell turned toward the world around him was essential to establishing himself as the ultimate arbiter of fashion – only he was sufficienty cool as to be seemingly unconcerned with what other men were wearing or doing. Brummell's dispassionate, impenetrable façade epitomized the priority of the external over the internal, of appearance over essence. Or rather, in Brummell's carefully calculated style, appearance became essence. The self-absorbed indifference that became the hallmark of dandyism during an age of desire allowed the observing public to transpose their own desires onto the dandy's fastidiously prepared canvas. This is the true source of originality in dandyism that Baudelaire mistakenly attributed to a specious aristocracy of the soul. The literary critic René Girard has captured this fundamental, modern aspect of dandyism:

> The dandy is distinguished by his affectation of cold indifference. But his is not the coldness of the stoic; it is calculated to stir up desire, a coldness which is always saying to the Others: "I am self-sufficient." The dandy wants to make Others imitate the desire he pretends to feel for himself. He exhibits his indifference in public places as one might draw a magnet through iron filings. He universalizes, industrializes asceticism for the sake of desire. There is nothing less aristocratic than this undertaking; it reveals the bourgeois soul of the dandy. This high-mannered Mephistopheles would like to be the capitalist of desire.[33]

Rather than a last vestige of a recently displaced aristocracy, as in Baudelaire's interpretation, dandyism can be seen as a first, pristine manifestation of the purposive interplay of fashion and desire as it evolves in a fully modern society. The cool indifference of the dandy has become institutionalized as one of the standard poses of the high-fashion model, for example.[34] It is also familiar in the studiously jaded manner affected by Andy Warhol's contingent of insiders in the New York hip society of the 1960s and their transformation into the *Interview* magazine denizens of the 1980s.

Brummell and Warhol adopted an attitude of self-absorption in order to sell themselves, to present their style as desirable in the eyes of others, while fashion models are posed so as to sell the commodities on or around their bodies. In truth, these are really the same thing. Fashion advertising, like much advertising in general, is selling a style of consumption, not only the particular goods contained within a photograph. The contemporary sellers of selves, particularly in the art world (unlike their dandy predecessors) also have products to sell, but do so by first hawking their personas.

Baudelaire expected the dandy to disappear as democracy spread its leveling tide, but the elitism of the dandy's style of consumption is in important respects a consequence of that tide. The relative permeability of social rank in modernity has created an environment in which the individual could hope to create his or her own identity, but as society becomes more egalitarian the desire to individuate oneself becomes more difficult to satisfy. The process of individuation is never autonomous; it requires the recognition of another person or a group. As we have seen, the anonymous quality of modernity nudges the individual toward external signs in order to be recognized, which necessitates the development of a common sign system. That means that the individual's choice of signs is circumscribed, limited by available permutations of the social code. Within that code, individual differentiation is always relative, being established through distinction from some other person or group.[35] So the identities of individuals, transmitted through external signs, are a function of the sign system itself and not expressions of essential qualities of autonomous subjects. Beau Brummell and Andy Warhol are able to distinguish themselves because they are adept at manipulating an existing code, not because the persona we see expressed in their style represents some genuine or authentic self that is unique.

The acceleration of changes in fashion noted by Simmel and Veblen is attributable to the instability built into the fashion code as a result of the relative character of positions within it. The struggle to establish one's identity and position is ceaseless because there are no objectively fixed statuses, but the struggle tends to reproduce the *de facto* statuses that do exist. The wealthier find it easier to shift their consumption from one set of objects to another than do those with less wealth. A competitive hierarchy is established, with no rest for anyone but with real upward movement forestalled – the dynamism of individual and group aspirations is thus institutionalized into a form of social stasis.[36]

The deep stability of the struggle for competitive identity is concealed by the sometimes frantic manipulation of appearances. Those at the top of the social order cast their glances sideways and downward, cultivating a style that appears natural and that imbues the objects that are signified within it as objects of intrinsic value. In the first instance, the fashionable objects of elite consumption serve as markers of group identity. Such objects may be located at either end of the temporal spectrum: they may be identified by their antiquity or by their newness. In either case, their authenticity or their timeliness will ensure their scarcity. With new objects governed by fashion, only an elite possesses, by self-determination, the requisite aesthetic sensibility to see them properly, at least in the short term. The severe quality of much modern design in interior decoration served this purpose particularly well. On the one hand, it represented in an extreme form the distinction between luxury and comfort noted earlier, relegating the latter to the level of vulgarity in the estimation of the fashionable while cloaking the luxurious in a disconcerting austerity initially incomprehensible to everyone else.[37] Jean Baudrillard catches the broader principle involved when he claims that

> beautiful, stylized, modern objects are subtly created (despite all reversed good faith) *in order not to be understood by the majority* – at least straight away. Their social function is first to be distinctive signs, to be objects which will distinguish those who distinguish them. Others will not even see them.[38] (Baudrillard's italics)

The first function of fashionable objects of this kind is therefore to distinguish "us" from "them" – it is a negative identity (we are not them) transmitted through an affirmative judgment (the sharing of good taste). As we have had occasion to remark before, good taste requires the abandonment of fashionable new objects once they have become common currency, and hence no longer marks of distinction, though it sometimes happens that the fashionable set, accustomed to the rapid changes in style necessitated by its precarious social lead, moves on to new styles without the old ones filtering down, which may be said to have been the case with modernism.[39]

Along with its stylistic acumen, the uppermost strata cultivates an appreciation of antiquities as a sign of taste but also as a sign of ancestry. Thus history is wedded to nature; the stylish not only

possess the seemingly natural ability to decipher newly coded
fashions but also possess a heritage. The age of an antique (and
frequently the lineage of its ownership) confers a legitimacy on its
possessor's taste – the owner, in Walter Benjamin's formulation,
shares in the aura of the unique original object.[40] This appropriation
of the past is a pseudo-aristocratic substitute for the fixed identity
conferred by family and rank in the prebourgeois era.

   For those below this upper crust – that is to say, for most everyone
– status identity requires a panoramic view. Identity is established
horizontally, but only in small part. More important are the views
upward and downward. Positions in the social order are most
precarious in the great middle of the middle class, where identity is
poised uneasily between relationally defined extremes and where
catching up to the styles previously adopted by those above
instantaneously results in the debasement of those same styles – the
accomplishments of high culture become middle-brow, designer
labels no longer carry a cachet of exclusivity.[41]

*

The obsession with lifestyle that is pervasive in the United States
today is attributable in part to the anxiety such social fluidity entails.
Television programs such as "Lifestyles of the rich and famous" or
"Entertainment Tonight," which focus on many of the same famous
rich, or any of the myriad spinoffs produced by local television
stations for inclusion between gameshows, are kitsch versions of the
emulative enterprise. *Architectural Digest, Art and Antiques*, the
principal fashion magazines, *Interview*, and a host of other publications advertise an image of more sophisticated lifestyles their readers
can either identify with or desire to possess. But these overt
purveyors of glamour and desire are merely the most obvious sources
of such emulative models; the media are saturated with them. The
New York Times can be taken as an example here. Aside from its
reporting on local, national, and international news, the *Times*
reports an implicit lifestyle to its upscale readers. There are of course
the daily advertisements for Brooks Brothers, Saks, Bloomingdale's,
Bonwit Teller, and other fashionable New York stores, which are
supplemented by fashion and society pages and topped off by the
Sunday magazine section, with its more elaborate advertising, and
special supplements on men's and women's seasonal fashions. But

there are also elaborately produced special Sunday supplements for home design, home entertaining, and travel. The New York edition contains a "Living Section" on Wednesdays and a "Home" section on Thursdays. New columns have been instituted with titles like "Life in the 30s," "About Men," and "Hers." The regular Sunday travel section contains reports from correspondents unself-consciously running up their expense accounts. All of these features purvey a code, a set of signs by which to live a certain kind of life. *Times* readers are expected to know the code and either confirm their image of themselves in it or recognize their aspirations through it.

This code is a sign system of consumption. The *Times* does not purposefully produce this code, it merely attempts to provide material that its particular readers find interesting and it provides it according to the values and style of culture it wittingly and unwittingly embodies. A series of examples drawn from a single issue of the paper conveys enough of what goes on here to see the code emerging. My examples are not drawn from any of the special supplements or sections, but from the second half of the news portion of the Sunday edition for October 5, 1986. The first item is a column entitled "New Yorkers, etc." that has as its particular subject this day the issue of what partners with dual careers do with their separate pay checks. The reporter summarizes the standard variations as follows:

> Some men and women pool whatever they earn, and some couples pool only a percentage of their income, retaining the rest for their own purposes. In certain cases, one salary pays all the routine bills, and the other is set aside for major expenses. Yet another arrangement is to have everything but luxuries come out of one person's salary, with the second income (depending on its state of health) going toward such things as a vacation, a fur coat, a second home or investments.[42]

One couple surveyed – both executives – pool their money, "but the disbursements come out of several joint accounts." Organized along corporate lines, the couple has "a separate partnership account for the real majors – a short list that takes in vacations, car and similar items." Among the items that apparently are not considered major are "routine monthly expenses – telephone, electricity, groceries, cleaners, laundry, department stores," as well as money for her children from a previous marriage, and "insurance, mortgage and investments." The other couples mentioned in the column: an actress and an actor; an actress and a corporate vice president; a law firm partner and a senior vice president of a New York bank; a restaurateur and a real estate broker; a productivity consultant and a coin dealer; a public relations director for a publisher and the production manager for the women's wear division of the ubiquitous Ralph Lauren. One woman (the banker) remarks that "as a general rule my husband tends to pay the household bills – rent, telephone, electricity, nurse."

The second column is called "Our Towns" and concerns shopping to outfit the babies of the baby boom generation. It carries a dateline from White Plains, a Westchester suburb of New York, and is written in an ironic tone that reaches its apogee when the reporter, introducing a shopper who is employing a calculator in looking for a stroller, remarks that "everything is more technical when it comes to modern babies, and thank heavens so many of today's mothers have Ph.D.'s or run corporations."[43] The reporter notes that "as is usual, a new generation of mothers has left the previous generation in the dust," then goes on to record the following exchange:

> "I'm amazed at all the things my daughter feels she needs for this little baby," said Lucy Nelson. "She wants the Kanga Rocka Roo."
> "And I want the little pouch," said her daughter, Mary McNally, who is seven months pregnant.
> "She wants the Fisher intercom system," said the mother.
> "We've heard Aprica is the Mercedes of strollers," said the daughter.

The generational theme is repeated in other guises. For one thing, "today's young parents are determined not to repeat the mistakes of their parents, so they spend hours reading Consumer Reports." In another instance, it is noted that, whereas "a decade ago, shoppers chose from a few types of vinyl bumper cushions to protect their babies from crib bars," the White Plains store "carries 70 different quilted cloth bumpers." And along with the modern parent/shopper there is the modern baby: "When it comes to the modern baby, the philosophy seems to be, 'Oh, why not.' 'If they make something,' said Lisa Kaplan, 'she should have it.'" Elsewhere:

> No one is happier about the fully equipped modern baby than the modern baby store owner. In 1973, when babies were totally out of

vogue, the Darling baby supply store here laid off workers and pulled a truck off the road. Now volume is three times what it was then. On Saturdays pregnant mothers stand belly to belly in the clogged aisles. On Thursday nights like this one, when the store is open late, husbands in gray suits and wives in their office maternity dresses rush here from work.

This excursion into modern baby consumption is best culminated by the description of a couple that follows the reporter's sartorial comment. The couple, presumably in gray suit and office maternity dress, have balked at the store's selection of quilted bumper cushions ("Is this all you have?"). The woman, only six months pregnant, explains that "We're having the room painted with Winnie the Pooh and the designer suggested getting the bumper color scheme first. . . . Then it'll be ready to paint." Her husband interjects, "People are going to think we're megayuppies." "Well we are," she says.

The last of the three examples also contains a reference to so-called yuppies, the 1980s appellation for a blatantly consumerist lifestyle. In this case, in an article appearing on the "Washington Talk" page about the emergence of various establishments in Washington, D.C. purveying "haute cuisine to go." These businesses "cater to the city's affluent as well as to the two-income couples who have more cash on their hands than time."[44] The idea that "no one has time to cook anymore," as it is put by the owner of one shop, is the key idea, but at least some of their clientele apparently have time to shop. The centerpiece of the story is the Sutton Place Gourmet, "a 17,000-square-foot food department store" located "in one of the city's wealthiest enclaves, a short distance from the high-priced homes of Foxhall Road and the quiet wealth of Embassy Row" that "has become a daily stop for many Washingtonians." When they arrive, they find the place

> filled with every imaginable fancy food, with prices to match: 600 kinds of cheese, 300 brands of imported beer, 11 varieties of dried mushrooms and six of truffles, seven kinds of foie gras and 22 of smoked fish, fresh herbs all year round, fresh bread and sweets and special dishes from an on-premises kitchen, lamb from Pennsylvania, butter from France, estate-bottled olive oil from Tuscany and wild rice from an Indian tribe in northern Wisconsin.

Among the many Washingtonians who regularly pass through are several celebrities – Lena Horne, Alexander Haig, Art Buchwald, and

George Bush (then Vice President), who "has been known to stop by in jogging attire to pick up some Scottish salmon." Thus the store becomes more than a store:

> "You can meet anyone there," says Sondra Gotlieb, wife of the Canadian Ambassador, Allan Gotlieb. "It's not like going to the supermarket. It's sort of like an entertainment, an adventure. People go in couples and wander about asking each other, 'Let's see, which one of these 18 different hams should we try today?'"

It is the Sutton Place Gourmet that the food and wine editor of the London *Guardian* is quoted as having described as "This yuppie-packed emporium." He did so, however, while comparing it favorably with Harrod's Food Hall, save for Harrod's superior architecture.

These three examples reveal a great deal – some of it obvious, some less so – about the lifestyle that is taken to be second nature by the writers, editors, and clientele (readers, advertisers) of this newspaper. The articles use different ways to establish a common identity between reader, reporter, and the people written about. The column names – "New Yorkers, etc." and "Our Towns" – and the section heading under which the third item appears – "Washington Talk" – convey an intimacy, a sense that what is being written and read about is "us." We can be anywhere – New York City, the suburbs, or even Washington – and still be united by a certain style of life. More than anything else, that style is defined by a mode of consumption that can treat investments, department store shopping, and domestic service as run-of-the-mill household expenses, comparable to rent or mortgage payments and utilities, while food bills normally include restaurants and prepared foods. Vacations and second homes are in the normal scheme of things. Above all else, the style of consumption is defined by an unlimited choice of goods on which to spend a large income – 600 kinds of cheese or 70 patterns of bumper cushions. Where scarcity exists in this lifestyle it is in an oft-noted insufficiency of time. For most people, making the money in order to consume on this scale requires what would likely be called a heavy investment of time, usually on the part of two persons. And then there is the time that goes into managing the requisite income so as to keep the consumption flowing evenly and without pause. Consuming all this stuff requires more time, as does the shopping itself, which entails taking the time to make a choice between all those different kinds of ham.[45] But the choice that is imposed here is not the choice involved in allocating scarce resources between alternative ends, as is the common assumption of the scarcity postulate in economics, but a choice that results from the sheer volume of alternatives. It is a choice induced by affluence.

The fact that dual-income couples have such a prominent presence in these articles is an indication that the style of consumption is what counts; the occupations that support it are an elaboration of that style. High-paying jobs predominate, mixing professional, cultural, and corporate/managerial occupations. Once, perhaps, the income from only one of these positions would have been enough to achieve the desired level of consumption; now it takes two. The articles leave the impression that being a part of a couple is a rational choice necessitated by the cost of consuming in the desired style: only neanderthals and the super rich forgo this choice.

On the cultural side, a certain kind of New York (read: sophisticated) culture predominates; the actor and actress couple who appear in the first article are appearing on the New York stage,[46] while the elegant Lena Horne makes a celebrity appearance in the food emporium, lending an air of artful good taste to the composite image. The exclusivity of the goods purveyed by the various stores – the Aprica strollers and abhorrence of vinyl displayed in White Plains, the wild rice from a northern Wisconsin Indian tribe at the gourmet supermarket – are also signs of distinctive taste. The placement of the Sutton Place Gourmet near Embassy Row in the reporter's description functions in a similar way and serves to give an indication of the social significance of its patrons. Yet these signs of exclusivity seem to jar with the notion that "many Washingtonians" shop at the food store and with the crowded conditions at the Westchester baby supply store. As for the gourmet supermarket, the author of the Washington story has to be wilfully ignorant of the class and racial composition of the capital in order to make such an assertion – in effect, she has reduced the city to an affluent neighborhood of its northwest section, rendering the vast majority of Washington, D.C.'s residents invisible. But this is what is required in codifying a lifestyle: it is an act of restriction, of inclusion and exclusion. From the point of view of those for whom society is thus encoded, those who are outside are unseen, but their presence is implicitly necessary for the described lifestyle's exclusivity. What the reporter really means is that many of "us" who live in Washington shop there.

The crowded baby store conveys a different and somewhat more complex message. In this article, the customers, though named, are not specifically identified in the same way as in the article on sharing expenses – none of the patrons is endowed with an occupational description. Instead, we are given loud clues as to their collective identity as trendy young upscale consumers who think of themselves as upscale. In a word, yuppies. The ironic tone of the article and its self-mocking subjects might provide the opportunity for those who do not see themselves within its coded orbit to shake their heads and say something disparaging about these single-minded hedonists. For others, however, the article provides the opportunity to laugh at oneself, to see oneself as part of a crowd of customers and, in laughing at the overtly conspicuous consumption, to legitimate one's own consumption style. The irony is an instrument through which the anxiety of seeking identity through possessions is relieved: we're not alone, we're all doing this crazy thing.[47]

But it is not all drudgery. There is an obvious delight in the shopping. Counterbalancing the rational, almost work-ethic Consumer Reports approach of the anonymous White Plains crowd is the pure sensuality and enjoyment conveyed in the description of the Sutton Park Gourmet, where shopping is an entertainment and an adventure. This is the enjoyable *flânerie* of the consumption ideal, the stroll through the aisles where the desirous foods intermingle with stylish and famous people. The person who articulates this ideal, however, is the one person identified in any of these articles who is herself without a job. Or rather, she is the one whose occupation it is to entertain and to be entertained: the Canadian Ambassador and his wife are pillars of the Washington social scene. There is thus a leisured ideal structuring this code that is brought fleetingly within touch during the act of shopping, only to be lost again on the way back to the office. Articles such as these keep that ideal before their readers, legitimating it and carrying them through to the next touch.

*

The consumption code of the upper-middle-class lifestyle conveyed by the *Times* has three implicit orientations. The first is horizontal: it provides information to people who are members of this coded group, or who are within striking distance of aspiring to it, and gives them the basis upon which to identify themselves and each other.

The second orientation is downward: the unseen but present Others who are far enough below that they are unable to read the nuances of the code but able to identify the signs that constitute it as conspicuous signs of wealth. The third orientation is upward; the leisured ideal that serves as the model of emulation. The constant reiteration of the two-income couple is thus a reinforcement of a group identity but also an ethical assertion akin in its function to the Protestant ethic. It conveys a general sense of having earned the goods that are meant to identify this style of life. But it also expresses a faint resentment toward the leisured who can consume in this style without working, while nevertheless adopting the image of their lifestyle as the model to be imitated.[48]

The ideal of the leisured class in the example we have been exploring performs the function of what René Girard has called the mediator of desire. In this formulation, a subject (whether a person or a class) does not spontaneously generate desires but rather adopts them via a model which is imitated. Sometimes the model is a mythic or literary figure or is otherwise outside the realm of existence of the imitating subject, and in that case there is what Girard calls external mediation. When the model is close enough to the subject to be a competitor for what is desired – when, in adopting the mediator's desires, the subject thus produces the mediator as a rival – he speaks of internal mediation.[49] In Girard's argument, internally mediated desire is characteristic of modernity (the novel is its literary form). Internal mediation is prevalent because of the fluidity of social strata and the egalitarian ideology that is coexistant with it, and because of the death of God. Lacking all other reference points, men and women look to each other as models to be imitated, but the proximity of those models means that there inevitably will be an element of envy and hatred, not least because the mediator will appear as a rival. Understood in this way, "democracy is one vast middle-class court where the courtiers are everywhere and the king is nowhere."[50]

Girard's theory of triangular desire captures some of the same qualities of the structure of desire in modernity as Adam Smith's notion of the spectator, discussed in chapter one. Smith's spectator can be seen as akin to Girard's external mediator since, as a hypothetical Other, the spectator's function is to act as an ideal referee in the game of distinction without participating in it. Where social inequality is deemed to be legitimate, this game can be played without excessive rancor, but once such legitimacy is seriously and continuously called into question, the game becomes more intense. Smith emphasized the second-order happiness the competition for social esteem brings and the material wealth it inadvertently generates, but as that competition intensifies, as the perspective of comparison narrows, it sows the seeds of perpetual frustration. Chasing an image of what we would like to be like, we are less likely to be satisfied with what we are at any moment. We resent those whom we cannot catch and those whom we perceive as trying to catch us. Consuming is the activity of a democracy of signs; resentment is its final judgment.

NOTES

1   Walter Benjamin, "Paris, capital of the nineteenth century," in *Charles Baudelaire: A Lyric Poet in the Era of High Capitalism*, trans. Harry Zohn (London: N.L.B, 1973), 154–76.

2   Johann Friedrich Geist, *Arcades: The History of a Building Type* (Cambridge, Mass.: MIT Press, 1983), 68-9.

3   Exoticism was particularly evident at the 1889 and 1900 exhibitions, during the hey-day of French imperialism, but was a feature of every exposition from 1867 on. See Rosalind H. Williams, *Dream Worlds: Mass Consumption in Late Nineteenth-Century France* (Berkeley and Los Angeles: University of California Press, 1982), 61.

4   Michael B. Miller, *The Bon Marché: Bourgeois Culture and the Department Store, 1869-1920* (Princeton: Princeton University Press, 1981), 42.

5   Sigfried Giedion, *Space, Time and Architecture: The Growth of a New Tradition*, 5th edn (Cambridge, Mass.: Harvard University Press, 1967), 238-41.

6   Norma Evanson, *Paris: A Century of Change, 1878-1978* (New Haven and London: Yale University Press, 1979), 141.

7   Another technical transformation that was part of this new spectacle of movement and display was the introduction of open elevators within the interior courts of the department stores. The first of these was introduced in the addition to Grands Magasins du Printemps around 1910. For a photograph of this interior, see Williams, *Dream Worlds*, figure 18.

8 Miller, *Bon Marché*, 24-5; Williams, *Dream Worlds*, 66-7.

9 Williams, *Dream Worlds*, 67.

10 Miller, *Bon Marché*, 61-2.

11 See the discussion in Miller, *Bon Marché*, 178-89.

12 Miller, *Bon Marché*, 36.

13 Geist, *Arcades*, 114.

14 Walter Benjamin, "The Paris of the Second Empire in Baudelaire," in *Charles Baudelaire*, 37:

> The arcades were a cross between a street and an *interieure*. . . . The street becomes a dwelling for the *flâneur*; he is as much at home among the facades of houses as a citizen is in his four walls. To him the shiny, enamelled signs of businesses are at least as good a wall ornament as an oil painting is to a bourgeois in his salon. The walls are the desk against which he presses his notebooks; news-stands are his libraries and the terraces of cafes are the balconies from which he looks down on his household after his work is done.

15 Benjamin, "The Paris of the Second Empire in Baudelaire," 36.

16 Charles Baudelaire, "The painter of modern life," *Selected Writings on Art and Artists*, trans. P. E. Charvet (Harmondsworth: Penguin Books, 1972), 499-500. The painter of the title is the illustrator Constantin Guys.

17 Baudelaire, "The painter of modern life," 403. For a discussion of fashion as a language system, see Marshall Sahlins, *Culture and Practical Reason* (Chicago: University of Chicago Press, 1978), 179-204.

18 For a discussion of aristocratic styles of consumption and their influence on the French middle classes, see Williams, *Dream Worlds*, 19-57.

19 The degree to which this comparison to palaces rings true can be seen in the practice instituted at the Bon Marché of guided tours of the store, including the behind-the-scenes offices, dormitories, and kitchens (Miller, *Bon Marché*, 169), mimicking the tours of art collections in English country houses that originated in the seventeenth century (see above, chap. 1, n. 29).

20 Williams, *Dream Worlds*, 102:

> No matter how desirable the item, no matter what its former associations with wealth, as soon as it becomes cheap enough to find a mass market it loses its rarity and therefore its

desirability.... The pleasure of the illusion of wealth disappears into the distance as the mass market keeps encroaching, transforming the rare into the commonplace. When everyone can afford an imitation or cheap Oriental rug, then people want a handmade tapestry. The genuine continues to signify wealth, and common people continue to suffer from the vision of unattainable merchandise. There can be no authentic democratization of luxury because by definition luxury is a form of consumption limited to a few. Modern society has instead introduced the proliferation of superfluity.

21 George Simmel, "Fashion," in *On Individuality and Social Forms*, ed. Donald N. Levine (Chicago: University of Chicago Press, 1971), 296.

22 Simmel, "Fashion," 299.

23 Simmel, "Fashion," 305: "It is peculiarly characteristic of fashion that it renders possible a social obedience, which at the same time is a form of individual differentiation; fashion does this because in its very nature it represents a standard that can never be accepted by all." That is, it cannot be accepted simultaneously by all.

24 Fashion thus represents in a clear way the organization of objects as signs in modernity. For a discussion that forms the basis of much of what follows, see Jean Baudrillard, *For a Critique of the Political Economy of the Sign*, trans. Charles Levin (St. Louis: Telos Press, 1981). See also Sahlins, *Culture and Practical Reason*.

25 Thorstein Veblen, *The Theory of the Leisure Class* (Harmondsworth: Penguin Books, 1979), 87. The point is made emphatically in Sahlins, *Culture and Practical Reason*, 203:

> The clothing system in particular replicates for Western society the functions of the so-called totemism. A sumptuary materialization of the principal coordinates of person and occasion, it becomes a vast scheme of communication – such as to serve as a language of everyday life among those who may well have no prior intercourse of acquaintance. 'Mere appearance' must be one of the most important forms of symbolic statement in Western civilization. For it is by appearances that civilization turns the basic contradiction of its construction into a miracle of existence: a cohesive society of perfect strangers. But in the event, its cohesion depends on

a *coherence* of specific kind: on the possibility of apprehending others, their social condition, and thereby their relation to oneself 'on first glance.'

26   Simmel, "Fashion," 311. W. F. Haug, *Critique of Commodity Aesthetics: Appearance, Sexuality and Advertising in Capitalist Society*, trans. Robert Bock (Minneapolis: University of Minnesota Press, 1986), 90, ascribes a similar role in fashion to rebellious youth subcultures, but without specifically noting the destructive quality at work.

27   On potlatch, see Marcel Mauss, *The Gift: Forms and Functions of Exchange in Archaic Societies*, trans. Ian Cunnison (New York: W. W. Norton, 1967). See also Baudrillard, *Critique of the Political Economy of the Sign*, 51-2; Georges Bataille, *The Accursed Share*, vol. 1, trans. Robert Hurley (New York: Zone Books, 1988), 63-77.

28   Veblen, *Theory of the Leisure Class*, 75, 176-7.

29   In the United States, such discomfort has been particularly evident in the critiques of the so-called hedonistic culture of modernity mounted by such figures as Daniel Bell and Irving Kristol. See Michael Rogin, "Pa Bell," *Salmagundi* 57 (Summer 1982): 145-58; Nicholas Xenos, "Neoconservatism Kristolized," *Salmagundi* 74-5 (Spring–Summer 1987): 138-49.

30   Quoted in James Harvey, "Screen gems," *New York Review of Books*, June 30, 1988, 24.

31   Baudelaire, "The painter of modern life," 420. For an account of Baudelaire's appropriation of dandyism and his personal difficulties in emulating the dandy's style, see Jerrold Seigel, *Bohemian Paris: Culture, Politics, and the Boundaries of Bourgeois Life, 1830-1930* (New York: Viking, Elisabeth Sifton Books, 1986), 97-109. Cf. Benjamin, "The Paris of the Second Empire in Baudelaire," 96-7.

32   Williams, *Dream Worlds*, chap. 4 contains an account of Brummell as well as of dandyism in France. On dandyism as a mode of consumption, cf. Colin Campbell, *The Romantic Ethic and the Spirit of Modern Consumerism* (Oxford: Basil Blackwell, 1987), 167-72.

33   René Girard, *Deceit, Desire, and the Novel: Self and Other in Literary Structure*, trans. Yvonne Freccero (Baltimore: Johns Hopkins University Press, 1965), 162. Girard is here drawing an explicit contrast between Baudelaire's interpretation of dandyism

and its treatment in the works of Stendhal and other nineteenth-century novelists.

34 Another typical pose, usually employed with women models but increasing common to both genders, involves having the model looking at him or herself in a mirror, inviting the viewer to share in a narcissistic revelry. For a discussion of this sort of advertising pose within the context of modern western art, see John Berger, *Ways of Seeing* (New York: Viking Press, A Richard Seaver Book, 1973).

35 This is the argument in Pierre Bourdieu, *Distinction: A Social Critique of the Judgement of Taste*, trans. Richard Nice (Cambridge, Mass.: Harvard University Press, 1984).

36 Baudrillard, *Critique of the Political Economy of the Sign*, 50: "As one is elevated on the social scale, objects multiply, diversify and are renewed. Their accelerated traffic (circulation) in the name of fashion quickly comes to signify and to present a social mobility that does not really exist." See also the discussion in Fred Hirsch, *Social Limits to Growth*, A Twentieth Century Fund Study (Cambridge, Mass.: Harvard University Press, 1978), chap. 1.

37 Witold Rybczynski, *Home: A Short History of an Idea* (New York: Viking, 1986), argues that comfort is an invention of bourgeois Europe, initiated in seventeenth-century Dutch interiors. He defends this value against the deliberately uncomfortable elitism of modernism as represented by Le Corbusier, Breuer, and Mies van der Rohe. Along the way, Rybczynski notes that Ralph Lauren makes millions designing elaborate furnishings that convey comfort for the upscale patrons of Bloomingdale's while reserving a modernist, minimalist interior decoration for his own upper Fifth Avenue duplex. But it seems to elude him that the more comfortable surroundings of authentic period pieces found in Malcolm Forbes' office are equally signs of elite distinction. For a vigorous aesthetic and moral defense of modernism, see the review by William H. Gass, "Making ourselves comfortable," *New York Times Book Review*, August 3, 1986.

38 Baudrillard, *Critique of the Political Economy of the Sign*, 48.

39 The point that modernism never really became as popular as its critics claim is made by Gass, "Making ourselves comfortable."

40 Walter Benjamin, "The work of art in the age of mechanical

reproduction," in *Illuminations*, trans. Harry Zohn (New York: Schocken, 1969), 217-51.

41   On middle-brow culture, see the discussion in Pierre Bourdieu, *Distinction*, chap. 6.

42   Enid Nemy, "New Yorkers, etc.," *New York Times*, October 5, 1986. It is assumed that some form of sharing is normal, since "it's almost unheard of for only one to foot all the bills, unless that one is so rich that offering to help would be ludicrous or, in the case of a man, so macho that the idea of a woman's contributing would send self-esteem staggering."

43   Michael Minerip, "Our towns: with a new baby boom, a buying boom," *New York Times*, October 5, 1986.

44   Barbara Gamarekian, "Getting fancy foods up to the competitive level," *New York Times*, October 5, 1986.

45   On the scarcity of time that results from consumption under conditions of affluence, see Staffan B. Lindner, *The Harried Leisure Class* (New York: Columbia University Press, 1970). See also the analysis in Hirsch, *Social Limits to Growth*, 72-7.

46   One of the actresses is Arlene Dahl, who had a long film career before turning to television. At the time of the article she had recently left her role on a T.V. soap opera, a genre that was shedding some of its vulgar connotations in favor of a new camp trendiness. In any event, the article describes her as "an actress and author" and points out that she left the series in order to write a novel.

47   A similar, though more overt, function is performed for a self-consciously flashier southern California audience in Ronald Brownstein and Nina J. Easton, "The new status seekers," *Los Angeles Times Magazine*, December 27, 1987/January 3, 1988. Also included in this issue is Rochelle Reed, "Objects of our desire," an itemized list of allegedly current status objects (Harley-Davidson motorcycles, Michael Graves-designed teapots) and practices (Australian vacations, the use of cash rather than credit cards in restaurants). I am indebted to John Goulding for bringing this issue to my attention.

48   Judith L. Goldstein, "Lifestyles of the rich and tyrannical," *The American Scholar* (Spring 1987): 235-47, reveals a similar sort of resentment by contrasting media coverage of the conspicuous consumption of Imelda Marcos (and, to a lesser extent, Michele Duvalier) with that of Malcolm Forbes. The *New York Times*

figures prominently here, too.

49 Girard, *Deceit, Desire, and the Novel*, 9.
50 Girard, *Deceit, Desire, and the Novel*, 119.

Conclusion

Affluent societies are affluent because they generate an endless stream of goods, not because they distribute them equitably. Within such a society there are gross inequalities that separate those at the top from those at the bottom to such a degree that they appear to belong to different societies, but between these extremes there are gradations of social standing that provide meaningful distinctions between people and groups and that constitute a coherent structure of relative status. These statuses are relative because they are not representative of some intrinsic quality, though the occupants of some of the higher ones often try to convince us otherwise by presenting themselves in the model of an imagined aristocracy. Status in modern affluent societies depends instead upon appearances, upon the distinctive signs that identify a person as belonging to a group by distinguishing that group from others whose signs, in turn, similarly identify them. These signs are objects, but the style in which these objects are displayed and consumed is equally a sign. We identify ourselves through these signs to a mass audience for whom we are otherwise anonymous.

Because these statuses are not fixed, there is a constant process of differentiation going on that is required for social identity. From the point of view specific to any given group, the signs of those above it in the social order will appear as signs of luxury and thus as objects to be desired. At the same time, maintaining status identity means differentiating oneself from those who are attempting to appropriate one's own signs, which is effected by appropriating new signs for oneself. This is a description of the familiar "Keeping up with the Joneses" syndrome, only writ large and continuously rewritten.

In such a social situation, individuals experience a world of insufficiency. Seeking to identify ourselves, we encounter myriad models for emulation, either on our travels through the public spaces of modernity – airports, avenues, stores – or through exposure to their film, print, video, or audio representations, or both. Whole industries dealing in fashion, advertising, and entertainment are devoted to keeping these images continually before us. Where there is enjoyment to be had in the pursuit of the desires we adopt along with these models, it lies not so much in the enjoyment of the things we accumulate – though there is that, if time allows – as in imagining ourselves as what we want to be through the possession of these things. But because the models change or are continuously revised, there is no respite from the travail of our imaginings; we never quite get to where we want to be.

The economizing logic of scarcity that we accept along with our perpetual frustration at not being able to have what we desire clashes with the logic of consumption upon which social identity is based. This is the bad conscience of modernity and it affects our attitude toward political power. The frustration at never seeming to catch up to those whose lifestyle we emulate can be chaneled in a nominally egalitarian direction through redistributional appeals to the state. Such appeals are attempts to reduce the distance between statuses by spreading wealth more evenly and by having the state provide services, particularly with regard to education, that are themselves signs of distinction when access to them is maintained unequally. But among the effects of these appeals is fear of losing ground to those below in the status order and of undermining one's own ability to distinguish oneself. So state policies that appear at one moment as legitimate and fair because they are universal and thus benefit oneself seem the next moment to be special pleading and unfair because they benefit those with whom one is in status competition.[1] In the latter case, this reaction is likely to take the form of a moral appeal to the state to act as a disciplinary power, to impose an economizing reason upon those who are further down on the social order. Middle-class support for and subsequent reaction against the welfare state can thus be interpreted as having a common source in a view of the state as a guarantor of status.[2]

Rather than alleviating the frustrations of desire the welfare state accelerates them. We are no more willing than Hobbes's readers to fully accept the notion of autorepression; claiming that we all need a dose of discipline is an easy solution when in practice the disciplinary cages are to be lowered upon others. Rousseau's proposal of a moral revolution from above to free us from our self-imposed social scarcity is not of much appeal either. The Chinese Cultural Revolution gave us a look at what that process might look like when carried out in earnest; only the imagination can provide the horrific details that would accompany such a project under conditions of modernity.

The moral revolution from below that characterizes the Romantic response to the sources of scarcity, also a legacy of Rousseau, appears equally doomed, though for less overtly frightening reasons. This road would circumvent the frustrations of modernity and avoid an appeal to the state by withdrawal from the logic of scarcity and the imperatives of consumption. It is in many ways an attractive alternative, but the difficulties entailed in fashioning an authentic self amidst the sign system of identity and recognition in which we live are obvious. They were well enough known to Rousseau in his *Emile* where, paradoxically but necessarily, only the constant presence of the tutor could ensure Emile's autonomy. They were known, too, to Baudelaire, who hoped in vain to find such an authentic self in the demeanor of the dandy. But doomed as it may be to an underground existence as a nagging negation of the status quo, the Romantic impulse is the only tradition within modernity that is capable of grasping all that is entailed in our presupposition of universal scarcity. Perhaps the best we can hope for is to free our minds from this concept that has taken hold of it, but such understanding is the first stage of freedom from our self-imposed slavery.

NOTES

1   This may help to provide the interpretive framework for explaining an example regarding public goods offered by Claus Offe, "Democracy against the welfare state?," *Political Theory* 15, no. 4 (November 1987):

> If, in the course of social change, existing notions of sameness come under strain and stress, the seemingly self-evident public good undergoes a Gestalt-switch and turns into the object and outcome of a distributive game. Before his switch occurs, a social policy, say the introduction of unemployment

insurance, will be generally discussed and perceived in terms such as the creation of a just society, the guarantee of peaceful industrial relations, or the maintenance of aggregate demand. But *after* the switch, the very same policy will be viewed in categories of equivalence, exploitation, and redistribution, for example, in terms of inappropriate burdens being imposed on the industrious and active parts of the work force, and of undeserved benefits being granted to the unemployed. . . . In all such cases, the decisive change is not on the level of objective events and facts, but on the level of interpretive frameworks and the strategic adoption of beliefs and expectations.

2   This is one of the arguments that emerges in Fred Hirsch, *Social Limits to Growth*, A Twentieth Century Fund Study (Cambridge, Mass.: Harvard University Press, 1976).

Index

abundance 57, 64 (50n); desire for
  53–4; false promise of 67; future of
  51–2; Mill's vision of 44; notion of
  35, 37
advertising, in eighteenth century
  9–10; and fashion 98
affluence, and choice 1–2; paradox of
  1, 67; reasons for 115
Appleby, Joyce, on scarcity 28–9
  (11n)
arcades 88–9, 109 (14n)

Bagehot, Walter 84 (26n)
Barbon, Nicholas, on want and desire
  29 (13n)
Baudelaire, Charles 89, 98; and
  dandyism 117; "The painter of
  modern life", quoted 89
Baudrillard, Jean, on modern objects
  99
Benjamin, Walter 7, 85, 100
Bentham, Jeremy 39, 45
birth control 39–40
Boileau, L. A. 86
Bon Marché 85, 86–7, 88
boulevards 88–9
Boulton, Matthew 9–10
Brakelond, Jocelyn of 55
Brummel, Beau 96–7, 98
Burke, Edmund 38, 57; Thoughts and
  Details on Scarcity 38

capitalism 49, 51, 52–3, 64 (50n)
Carlyle, Thomas 39, 54; notion of
  society 57; Past and Present 54–5

  on wealth 55
Chinese Cultural Revolution 117
choice, and affluence 1–2
Cobbet, William 57
Cohen, G. A., on abundance 53
comfort, defended 112 (37n)
commodity fetishism 85, 86
communism 49, 50–1, 53, 72
competition 42; emulative, 17, 26,
  45, 46
Condorcet, Marquis de 38
consumption 56, 80; in eighteenth
  century 8–10; emulative 37;
  patterns of 73; sign systems of
  101–8
cost-benefit analysis, 80

Dahl, Arlene 113 (46n)
dandyism 97–8, 117
demand, elasticity of 9, 10
desire 87; and acquisitiveness 19;
  emulative 13, 16, 45, 47; and
  Hobbes 4–5; and marginal utility
  theory 69–70, 73; mediator of 107;
  and recognition 13, 16; and
  Rousseau 23–4; and Scottish
  Enlightenment 11–12; triangular
  107–8; and welfare state 116

economic development 42–3
economic rationality 77–8
education 59 (8n); importance of
  39–40, 41–2, 43
Eiffel, Gustav 86
Elias, Norbert, quoted 32 (43n)

emulation, vertical and horizontal
  19, 90–1; *see also* social emulation
environment, creation of, in Paris
  85–7
esteem 8

famine 75
fashion 87, 89–90; advertising of 98;
  and objects 99; publications 100–1;
  social role of 91–5; spread of 8
Ferguson, Adam 11; on republican
  government 31–2 (37n)
flâneur 89
French Revolution, importance of
  35–6

Girard, René, on dandyism 97; on
  desire 107–8
Godwin, William 38
goods 81 (4n), 82 (12n);
  desirability of 109–10 (20n)
Gothic architecture 55, 56, 65 (63n)
Grant, Cary 95–6
Great Exhibition (1851) 37
Greeks, as inspiration for Ruskin 56;
  and scarcity, 3

happiness, 25, 34 (60n); and wealth,
  15
Haussmann, Baron 88–9
history, Marx's view of 48; and
  Romantic radicals 54, 57
Hobbes, Thomas 4
Hobsbawm, Eric 37
human behaviour, and scarcity 2
Hume, David, on comparison 32
  (37n); on emulation 19; on esteem
  18; as inventor of scarcity 20–1; on
  justice 20, 33, 38; on need and
  desire 11–12; and Rousseau 21; on
  sympathy 13–14, 32 (37n); *A
  Treatise of Human Nature* 20
hunters and gatherers, and scarcity,
  2–3

individual, and multiplicity of wants
  69–71, 73
individuation 98, 100
insufficiency, condition of 1, 2, 3
Interview 97, 100

Jevons, William Stanley 68

justice 20, 33, 38

Kadish, Alon, *The Oxford
  Economists in the Late Nineteenth
  Century* 77
Keynes, John Maynard, and need for
  recognition 45–7

labour 56; division of 72–3
lifestyle, examples of 101–5, 106–7
London, and invention of scarcity
  7–8
luxury 36–7; signs of 90–1

mail-order catalogues 88
Malthus, Thomas Robert, on
  education 59 (8n); *Essay on the
  Principle of Population* 38; and
  morality, 39–40; population
  principle, 38–9, 47
Mandeville, Bernard 13; *Fable of the
  Bees: or, Private Vices, Publick
  Benefits, The* 13
Marcuse, Herbert 53–4
marginal utility theory 68, 69–71, 73;
  76–7, 80, 81 (6n), 82–3 (18n)
market systems 74–5
marketing, importance of 28 (10n)
Marshall, Alfred, and marginal
  utility theory 69, 73; *Principles of
  Economics* 69
Marx, Karl, *Capital* 52; *Communist
  Manifesto* 51; *Economic and
  Philosophical Manuscripts* 49, 51;
  The German Ideology 48, 51; on
  history 48; on need 48–52; and
  population theory 47–8, 62(35n);
  Wage Labour and Capital 52,
  quoted 53
Menger, Carl, on human needs 71,
  73; *Principles of Economics* 68;
  and scarcity postulate 68–9
Mill, John Stuart 39, 40;
  Autobiography 44–5; on
  civilization 40–1; on education
  41–2, 43; on population 59–60
  (10n); and social development
  44–5; stationary state theory 40,
  43–4, 60 (12n)
money, importance of 74–5
Morris, William 55; *News from
  Nowhere* 55

necessity 43

needs 64 (55n), 64–5 (57n); absolute 1; authentic 50, 52, 53–4; conception of 4–5, 46–7; human 71, 73; manipulated 50; Marx's view of 48–52; neoclassical theory of 70–1; relative 1; satisfaction of 68; and Scottish Enlightenment 11–12; and society 22

neoclassical economic theory 70–5

noble savage 22, 23, 24

Offe Claus 117–18

Paris, creation of 85–7, 88–9

Paris Commune (1871) 88

Philosophic Radicals 39

Polanyi, Karl, on the term 'economic' 75–6

population principle 38–9, 47–8, 59–60 (10n), 62 (35n)

poverty, paradox of 37, 55

progress, concept of 35

rationality, various 77–9, 80–1

recognition, need for 45–7

rent and interest 82 (9n)

reputation, notion of 19

retailing, innovations in 87–8

Ricardo, David 43

Robbins, Lionel 68; quoted 2

Romantic radicals 54; and competion 56; and medieval inspiration 55–6, 57; and scarcity 58, 117

Rousseau, Jean-Jacques 42, 117; on desire 23–4; *Discourse on the Origin and the Foundations of Inequality among Men*, quoted 23–4; *Discourse on the Sciences and Arts* 21, quoted 22; *Emile, or On Education* 25, 26, 117; quoted 33–4 (60n); and Hume 21; on self 24–5; *The Social Contract* 25, 42; on social scarcity 22, 25–6

Ruskin, John 55, on labour and consumption 56; "Political economy of art" 56; *The Stones of Venice* 55; *Unto the Last* 57

Sahlins, Marshall, quoted 2, 3

St. George's Guild 57, 65 (65n)

Sartre, Jean-Paul, and scarcity 1

scarcity 64 (50n); 81 (4n); as an abstraction 28–9 (11n); cyclical 10; deliverance from 35; etymology of 3; and human development 1, 2; and Hume 20–1; invention of 7; logic of 79–81, 116; perpetual 10–11; and Romantic radicals 57, 58, 117; and Rousseau 22, 25–6; and signifiers of status 94–5; as technical concept 68–9; theory of 8, 75, 76; transcendence of 53

Scottish Enlightenment 11

self, and Rousseau 24–5

Sen, Amartya K. 75

Simmel, George, on fashion 91–2, 93

Smith, Adam 56; and division of labour 72–3; on need and desire 11; *The Theory of Moral Sentiments*, quoted 14, 15, 30–1 (26n); *Wealth of Nations* 36; on wealth 14–15

social development 44–5

social emulation 19, 20, 26–7, 46, 94, 95–6; and desire 13; in eighteenth century 9–10

social esteem, and Rousseau 24

social order 16–18; paradoxes of 36–7

society, and need 22

stationary state, theory of 40, 43–4, 60 (12n)

status 90; competition 46; recognition 18; signifiers of 93, 95, 115–16

style, as defined by consumption 104–5

stylish persona, examples of 96–9

sympathy 30–1 (26n), 32 (41n); notion of 13–14

taste, theory of 12–13

Taylor, Harriet 45

Times, New York examples from 101–5

Tocqueville, Alexis de 41; *Democracy in America* 41

totemism 110–11 (25n)

trade, benefits of 12

Veblen, Thorstein, on fashion 92–3; and marginalism 80; quoted 20; *Theory of the Leisure Class*, quoted 20, 93

wages 53
Walras, Leon 68
Warhol, Andy 97–8
wealth 13–15, 71, 92, 94; Carlyle's view on 55; desire for 41; and distinction 27; new definition of 28 (5n)
Weber, Max, on economic rationality 77–8, 79; *The Protestant Ethic and the Spirit of Capitalism* 79, 94

Wedgwood, Josiah 9–10
welfare state, and desire 116
Williams, Rosalind 87
world expositions 85

yuppies 103, 104, 105